D1634061

# The Year of Open Doors

**CARGO**

Cargo Publishing (UK) Ltd
Reg. No. 376700
www.cargopublishing.com

©2010 Cargo Publishing (UK) Ltd
and the individual contributors

"The Year of Open Doors"
Ed. Dr. Rodge Glass
ISBN-13 978-0-9563083-2-0
BIC Code-
FA Modern and contemporary fiction (post c. 1945)
FYB Short Stories

CIP Record is available from the British Library

First Published in the UK 2010
Published By Cargo Publishing
Printed in Great Britain by the MPG Books Group,
Bodmin and King's Lynn

Produced in association with:

PSYBT
The University of Strathclyde English Studies Department

For The Cargo Interns

# Contents

# INTRODUCTION

### Rodge Glass

I first met Mark Buckland in Autumn 2008. Shortly before that I'd finished a book which was partly about my apprenticeship as a writer, and once it was published I thought I should finally grow up, iron a shirt for once and start working with young writers in the same tradition I'd benefited from. I'd been an English undergraduate at Strathclyde University and a Creative Writing Masters student between there and Glasgow University, so I was pleased to return as Keith Wright Creative Writing Fellow at Strathclyde in September 2008. This allowed me to continue my own writing, and set up shop in the little office at the end of the corridor where I'd taken my first short stories to the then Writer in Residence, Robert Alan Jamieson, nearly a decade before.

At Strathclyde I found many promising, keen students who were anxious to practice their writing, build confidence, and steadily develop their literary voices. Mark was not one of them. He was certainly one of the most talented through my door, but he also exhuded a kind of confidence, an arrogance that set him apart. We discussed a couple of his stories and I was pleased to do it, but got the impression he visited mostly to introduce himself, to let me know he was warming up. He came to see me three times in a whole year during my Writer in Residence office hours, with the same stories. Meanwhile, I heard that he hadn't turn up to some classes, and had been known to storm out of others on principle. (The principle in question remained a mystery.) Aspects of Mark's personality reminded me of the kind of person I wished I'd been at 21 years old – so naturally, I wasn't entirely sure I liked him.

I didn't see Mark much then, but he did represent the Department of English Studies at Glasgow's Book Festival in March 2009, again giving off this strange sense of sureness, as if none of this was new to him. (It turned out, it wasn't. He'd been signed up by a literary representative five years earlier and very nearly had a teenage literary career.) A few months later, he won Strathclyde's Keith Wright Creative Writing Competition for the second time – all this with the same material I'd seen months before. I was beginning to suspect he'd written nothing else. Soon after, I discovered he had been running club nights and live literature nights around Glasgow for years, all under the same banner. I didn't think too much of this until he got in contact in late summer to announce that after graduation, in the midst of a global recession and with books chains and independents dying all over the UK, he'd set up a publisher called Cargo. He also mentioned that he wanted to publish my next novel. I asked him if he was rich and well connected. He laughed and told me, 'Not yet.' 'Well then,' I replied, 'I'm not sure about that. But there is something I've always wanted to do...'

     A couple of years before, Alan Bissett and I had talked about jointly editing a collection of new Scottish fiction in the tradition of *Lean Tales* (the 1985 book featuring stories by Alasdair Gray, James Kelman and Agnes Owens) and especially *Children of Albion Rovers*, a 1997 collection published by Rebel Inc. which featured then-emerging writers such as Irvine Welsh, Alan Warner and Laura Hird. Both of us had been excited as young writers by that can-do, art-before-money, independent spirit, driven by the likes of Kevin Williamson (editor of *Children of Albion Rovers* and of the Rebel Inc. magazine), who took publishing risks and supported underground literature. Alan and I drew up a list of possible writers, concentrating on newer names not included in the usual roll call considered important by literary critics, but who had voices we felt deserved to be heard. As an outsider to this tradition myself I was particularly interested in breaking apart this notion of what counted, and including writers from elsewhere who had made Scotland their home. The very fact that writers from other places now chose to do this contrasted sharply with the Scottish publishing landscape of the 1960s and 70s, which Edwin Morgan once compared to a wasteland. Our book was initially going to be called *Thi Six a Clock Nyooz*, named after Tom Leonard's fiery poem, but a bit of Scots was too much for London publishing houses; we later considered 'Open the Doors', a slight reworking of the more assertive 'Open the Door!', the Catherine Carswell novel published in 1920. We wanted a title that sounded positive and individual, without being soft.

This book Alan and I imagined nearly came to be, and was considered by several major publishers – all liked the idea but asked for a fistful of more established names to help sell it. We both felt this went against the spirit of the collection. I loved the writing of, say, Janice Galloway and Ali Smith and AL Kennedy, of Irvine Welsh and Andrew O'Hagan and Jackie Kay – but these were major writers of a different generation who'd inspired us, and who, crucially, were already hugely critically acclaimed. Our way was not considered commercial enough, and the idea for the collection fizzled out. That is, until I mentioned it to Mark.

By now it had evolved. I told him I wanted this collection to be internationalist, to have no age limit, to cap writers at maybe three or four full-length publications, and to feature newly commissioned stories with a contemporary setting. A good number of these writers should be short story specialists. I also asked that each be paid equally, the important thing being not the figure itself but that the book had no hierarchy. Mark agreed to all this, and said it was exactly what he wanted anyway. I was warming to my ex-student, who was now my new boss. We sat in a coffee shop in Shawlands, near to our homes, and joked over coffee about how it would all go horribly wrong. We'd probably end up suing each other, we said. Which sounded like fun.

This was Autumn 2009. By now Alan Bissett was a hugely busy performer of his own work who was looking forward to time off from prose to tour his recent plays. Also, he was co-Editor of *New Writing Scotland*, along with Carl MacDougall – more than enough reading for any man. So I invited Alan to be the first in my collection and decided to edit

the book alone but agreed to make all further decisions
jointly with Mark, which meant choosing who would get in
the book and how. We agreed suspiciously often. Mark was
no pushover, and was extremely business-like, far more than
me, but luckily we saw the book the same way, though our
stylistic preferences were very different – I was more of a
Carver man, he was an admirer of Borges. I was always looking to use less words, more ordinary words. Mark wanted the
opposite. We were going to enjoy fighting over which were the
best new(ish) writers in the country.

After drawing up a wish list, and a whole bunch of recommendations for each other, it became obvious there were
now far too many writers in Scotland who interested us. Our
favourites made enough for three books, and we had plenty
of homework reading to give each other too. So we agreed to
split the book into two sections:

1 -  Published writers we were both passionate about –
any single vote counted for nothing.

and

2 – Unknown writers, or ones with very little publica-
tion history. These writers might have a single short story
published, or a couple of pieces for radio. They might be
mainly performers of their work. They might have nothing so
far. Again, we both had to agree.

This divide meant sending out some invitations
(thankfully, only one writer politely refused, an acclaimed
poet not quite ready to publish prose), and we began a na-
tionwide search for undiscovered talent. This led to a mountain of applications, originally sifted through by Mark's
growing band of interns all as young and as keen and as in-
timidatingly intelligent as him. One of these, David Flood,
became my highly self-confident, well-read Editor's Assis-
tant. And so the project grew, and progressed, and grew
again.

We settled on a title, *The Year of Open Doors\**, a kind of descendent of the original, and Mark gave me freedom to pursue meaningful collaborations, such as an audio album version released by another great Scottish independent, **Chemikal Underground Records**. Meanwhile, the writers in *The Year of Open Doors* were given only a few restrictions. They were asked to write something on the topic – Scotland: Now. So what did we get?

What we got was an inspiring selection of stories dealing with a wide variety of subjects, settings and concerns, also a variety of literary approaches. Hardly surprising considering that along with writers from places as diverse as Falkirk, Lewis, Glasgow, Orkney, Dundee, Aberdeen and Edinburgh, The Year of Open Doors also features the work of writers who have come to these isles from Zimbabwe, South Africa, Bulgaria, Canada and the United States, via places as far apart as England and New Zealand. In a world where free movement over planet earth is often considered suspicious and borders believed to be sacred, I consider this diversity a major plus. And I'm pleased to have stories dealing with topics as disparate as the Asian Tsunami of 2004 **(Kevin MacNeil)**, a drugged-up club night on the Clyde **(Suhayl Saadi)**, Christmas day far from home for a lonely Indian girl **(Colette Paul)**, as well as a fine example of politically-spiked corporate noir at one end of the subject spectrum **(Sophie Cooke)** and a quiet island tale about building gates at the other **(Daibidh Martin)**. Commissioning new work was a risk. Receiving it was a pleasure.

---

*This came from a line spoken to another inspiring young man I met in 2008, called Damilola Ajagbonna-Xavier. Dami was a role model and mentor of other students who received an award for charity work from the Bishop of London, but who was then fighting extradition. He was eventually allowed to return, but before his appeal to remain in the UK and accept a place at Cambridge University was refused by the Home Secretary, his Pastor predicted that the year to come would be 'the year of open doors'. I'm grateful to Dami for letting me use the phrase to title our book.

We found writers for this book in many places. From sparky live literature nights like DiScomBoBuLaTe **(Kirstin Innes, Anneliese Mackintosh)** and Seeds of Thought **(Tawona Sitholé)**, from evangelical recommendations via other writers **(Nora Chassler, Jason Donald)**, from reading their books and tracking them down **(Kapka Kassabova)** as well as from our anonymous competition **(Helen Lynch, Allan Wilson and Micaela Maftei)**. Some of the writers here exist in several literary forms, as well other art forms **(Aidan Moffat, Doug Johnstone)**, and some are returning to prose for the first time in a while – there was one particular kindred spirit we wanted to steal back for fiction, someone who had also been a key figure in Scottish publishing with Clocktower Press **(Duncan McLean)**. And finally, we wanted an opening poem to bring out the flavour of the whole soup, and for that job we employed the charismatic Reader In Residence of the Scottish Poetry Library **(Ryan Van Winkle)**, also known for performance nights and independent publishing, this time on the East coast. Scotland is culturally diverse, but small. If you hang around for long enough, you tend to cross most of the talent at one time or another, or at least hear about it. Still, this is no clique collection. There are people here I have never met, and many I hardly know. That's the way it should be.

Perhaps some of the writers in this collection will leave Scotland someday. Perhaps some of them will do it soon. Perhaps some of the Scottish-born ones will emigrate – it doesn't matter, they'll still belong in this book. Because though it contains many Scots who are rightly proud of the rich literary and cultural history here, also a good number directly inspired by the work of previous generations, *The Year of Open Doors* isn't about trying to claim these writers for a Scottish cause, or fit them into an academic tradition where so-and-so begat so-and-so and all is tidy. We're not heading off on a well-funded government tour to advertise a nation, defined by tired clichés. We're interested in these writers giving a snapshot of here, now, suggesting something of Scotland's place in the world and how it has changed, also how the literary landscape has changed, as well as the makeup of the population. Because, like any confident, forward-looking country, Scotland is multicultural.

In my research for this book I read the introductions to several other short story collections. Usually these were based around some tenuous metaphor ('in many ways, a good short story collection is like a box of chocolates/trip to the zoo/walk on a circus high wire'), or were used as a platform to make a great proclamation. With this one the temptation is to say: here lies the future of Scottish Literature! Here are some of the finest writers of their generation! And I believe that's true – but it's for readers to decide, not me. I've read each of these stories so many times, and sometimes in so many versions that I love each of them with the bias of a parent who thinks their children are the cleverest, most beautiful, most promising in their class. I'm an evangelical supporter of every single writer represented here, and proud to be. But I'm not qualified to judge. So here's *The Year of Open Doors* – me, Mark, David and all at Cargo who have worked (mostly for nothing) to make this book happen hope you like it.

Speaking just for myself now, I'm not interested in borders. I'm not interested in flags or national anthems or pretending the little corner of the globe I live in is better than any place else. But I am interested in trying to make something tasty from local ingredients. In not waiting for permission to get started. Alasdair Gray famously called this working as if you live in the early days of a better nation. It's funny that this quote from the proud plagiariser is actually a rephrasing of a line from a poem first published in 1972 by the great Canadian poet, Dennis Lee - *"And best of all is finding a place to be / in the early years of a better civilisation."*\*

---

\*Dr Nicholas Bradley of the University of Victoria, Canada explains: 'There are a couple of lines in the ninth elegy of Lee's 'Civil Elegies' that are very similar to Gray's: "And best of all is finding a place to be / in the early years of a better civilisation."' (p50, Civil Elegies and Other Poems, Anansi, 1994).

Gray had often reminded folks publicly that the sentiment was not his, but after some years, forgot to keep mentioning it. And so, something previously Canadian became the quote outside the Scottish Parliament building, attributed to a famous literary Scotsman.

As I sit here writing this drinking a cool, French beer in a café in sunny Canada (I've been stranded here for a while by the Icelandic volcano) there's something about that I like.

**RG, Montreal, March 2010.**

**A SHORT STORY COLLECTION IS A JOINT EFFORT**

# THE YEAR OF OPEN DOORS

## One Year The Door Will Open

### Ryan Van Winkle

Door, I have knocked, pushed,
licked and, for a year, stroked
your veins smooth as varnish.
My knuckles are hard, black beetles.
    We were children first
    when I saw your blue sway
    into a cottage on the coast.
    Each day the repetitive,
    constant sea sneaking close.
Door, you have been painted many things;
argument red, family yellow, divorce brown.
I too have been locked and pushed
shut, hung on frames and forced to gaze
through creaking day and slamming night,
at the parked silver car and children
high on birch. Door, I too have stared
at my own brass, have become wood
    and squeaked with need. Weathered, pale,
    but still here. So we can peer through gloom
    and into each other, honest as hinge
    and nail, can open and call this home.

## United Solutions

## Sophie Cooke

---

**008632159**
**DATE OF RECORDING: 03.05.10**
**AMENDED: 01.08.10**

*Transcript reflects amendments made to original record-ing as per your request; WN's speech only.*

*JH.*

---

I'm Wesley. I'm your Campaign Advisor.

Everyone gets one. Ever since the unfortunate affair with Robert King.

Aye, that's right. The sex addict.

Ha ha! No, you're all right. It's more to explain how things work.

Of course. Still. We thought it might help. Coffee, tea?

Two Americanos, Gloria.

Okay. So. The trouble is, with the system of employee election for the Directorship -

Part of the brand, of course. But still a little problematic. From your point of view.

Aye, but, Mr McDowell, it is not enough for you to be the best candidate for the post. You might say that was second-ary. What matters most is that you can convince the employ-ees to elect you to the post.

Okay: Fraser. Thank you. And I'm glad of your confidence. May I say also, I think it is not unfounded. The thing is, there are certain things that some candidates do not neces-sarily understand. Specific things which must be understood by anyone applying for Directorship. After the unfortunate affair with Robert King, we feel it is necessary to spell these out.

Naturally. But I'm thinking more along the lines of... Let me explain. Directorship selection is an expensive process. The company, having so many millions of employees, is costly to reach. There must be selection posters and leaflets in every office, office car park, canteen... There must be personalised e-mails and a campaign in the wider press - not just news-paper coverage, but also radio and television. Further, you will need image advisors, speech-writers, a dedicated PR team to feed positive stories to the press - counteract any negative stories. Crisis man. Crisis management. And astro-turfing too.

Ha ha! No. No, it's when we organise a false grassroots move-ment -

Mm, isn't it - to blog and comment on websites. Really, you hadn't heard of it?

Er, Fraser. There's no need for all this with *me*.

Well. As you wish. So. Our people leave comments in the message threads. That's really it. Really -

Aye, very nicely put. 'Noms de plume.'

Yes, yes of course. What I'm saying is, this campaign - and all the carefulness about which you are so rightly concerned, Fraser - costs money. It would be wrong for us to offer Company funds to applicants. We can not have our employees funding the campaigns of applicants who they have not yet chosen to support. It goes against the grain of the whole brand. Each of you is being given a Campaign Advisor this year, in light of what happened with Robert King, but our main role is to safeguard the principles enshrined in the Directorship Selection process, rather than to offer you any competitive advantage over the other applicants. Having said that, of course I -

What? You are not on television, Fraser! Will you please drop the PC lingo, before you start making me nervous! 'Employee Choice' means, among other things, that applicants for the post of Director must find their own campaign funding.

Good. Is it hot in here? You look a bit hot. Nice room Henry has, but he keeps it a bit warm, no? Not too sure I fancy his taste in artwork, either. What's this meant to be? 'Girl confused by chilli peppers'?

Oh, is *that* what it is. Ah yes. I can see it myself now. You must have a good eye for modern art, Fraser.

No, no, you do. See, to me that just looks like a pile of aerated red crap. Are you hot, Fraser? You look a wee bit flushed. A wee bit red. I'll just open –

the...

There. That's better. Now. Where were we?

Funding, yes.

Thank you, Gloria.

You can receive donations to your campaign fund from any United Solutions employee. You can not receive donations from anyone outside of the Company. That would contradict the 'Employee Choice' principle. We can't have outside interests influencing the course of our selection process.

Ha! That's better! Here, I've drawn up a list of your necessary campaign expenditure. As you can see, it is all itemised, and all absolutely necessary. I'll give you a moment to - okay. And here is the amount which I, as your campaign manager, estimate you can raise through donations from your Company colleagues who support you.

Mmm. I imagine you are wondering how you can bridge it. Part of my role, Fraser, is to be that bridge.

*The Board.*

Because, Fraser, the excellent men and women who sit on our Board, also sit on the Boards of other companies. If you can convince the Board members that your policies as Director will benefit the other companies on whose Boards they sit, then naturally they will be able to gather funds for you from those companies.

No, no. It's all above board - no pun intended! The funds are donated via the Board members, who *are* employees of this Company.

Very simple. Sub-contracting.

Oh, anything. Any of the actions that the Company currently performs by itself, you can promise to sub-contract to one of the other companies. The last Director chose to sub-contract transport and construction. But really the field is wide open. Here, have a look - as you can see, there's plenty left - site security, staff training, staff healthcare, customer services, office cleaning, customer records storage and retrieval... Obviously, if you can promise, if you can assure another company that you will award them the contract for work currently done by United Solutions, then that company will be happy to fund your selection campaign - through their intermediaries who sit on our Board. The more you sub-contract, the stronger your position.

Of course there is! You can pick which things you want to be concerned about - for instance, office security, given the recent incidents with the cleaning ladies. Or perhaps, on a more, well, a softer note, the Company's environmental footprint. You decide which things you think the employees care about most, and then you talk a lot about these things. You draw their attention to everything that is not working in those areas at the moment, and you promise to improve things by sub-contracting the services to real experts - the 'professionals'.

Well, say you want to focus on internal security - why not promise to bring in dedicated private security teams from outside? Or if you want to focus on environmental issues, you can promise to bring in environmental consultants via a new eco-trust that the Board will set up. The key thing, the key thing Fraser is, that you make it clear the Company can't tackle the problem itself. Tell the employees that the current approach is just not working. Tell them things need to change - fast! Then show them just how able you are to change them, yes. You do *not* mention 'subsidies'. 'Partnerships' is the usual term. 'Harnessing innovation'. 'Attracting investment'. You want to make it sound like the other guys are the ones giving us the money, yes, not the other way round. 'A £50 million partnership to tackle climate change together: harnessing innovation, attracting investment.'

No, he didn't. I suggested it, but he...

Well thank you. Yes of course you can.

Anyway, my point is. You want to convince the employees that sub-contracting is a good idea in principle - but don't go into the maths. You can just focus on making the speeches. Very much your *forte*, that, isn't it. Motherwell was a triumph. The way you spoke about your childhood - moving, very moving. I could never carry a crowd like that. People often ask me why I've never been tempted to stand myself. Crowds, you see - we leave each other cold. Otherwise.

Ha! Yes, it 'creates jobs'. You know, hearing you speak, it almost convinces even me. You are a very convincing man. But, you know-

Of *course* you can.

Mm. I couldn't agree more.

Go on.

I'm so glad -

I'm glad to hear it.

Yes, wasn't that ridiculous. It never plays well in the long term. Obvious to everyone that what worked for the likes of Gandhi is substantially less becoming in today's corporate politician.

Loincloth! Ha, that's funny.

Oh! Ha! You're a funny man, Fraser.

What? Oh, nothing.

Nothing.

Look, Fraser. I'm on your team, okay? Relax. Heavens, man.

Okay. Good. So, you -

What do *I* think? Well, I agree with you, Fraser, naturally. So. The wider business community. You will cultivate your connections. It doesn't just have financial benefits, but also image benefits. Our employees see you shaking hands with the chairman of Nesco, they're not going to be suspicious: they're going to be reassured. Impressed. Want a look inside their heads? I can see inside their heads, Fraser, and I'll tell you what they think. 'If big businessmen and big managers respect Fraser McDowell, then so should small businessmen and small managers. So should I.'

I know, I know. Different creature altogether.

Obsessed with the balance books. Put a small businessman in charge of a big business, it'd collapse in three months flat. You know that, I know that. Too busy slaving away trying to turn a profit to notice the fucking massive blank cheque outside the window.

~~'In the lobby!'~~ Ha! That's good.

So, which policy areas would you like to focus on?

The *environment*. Excellent.

Yes of course, I'd be flattered. Now, any others? Remember, the more you –

- *employee healthcare*. Excellent.

Ah, no. That's very out of date now, Fraser. To be honest, it doesn't really matter what our balance of payments is, because if you borrow money from the right places, then – boom! More selection funding. So, best not to meddle with that. Besides, we can't very well sub-contract 'profitability', can we! Although maybe - well, let me look into it, actually.

Perhaps one of the Board members knows somebody who'd be willing to set up a subsidiary company and bid for it.

Advice. You could sub-contract business advisors. To help enhance Company profitability.

Yes, of course it would be expensive. Otherwise there'd hardly be any point, would there? As long as it doesn't work, though, it might be rather a good idea. We could outsource 'improving profitability', and still keep outsourcing the same levels of debt. Now, how about training? I happen to know -

Excellent. So. You'll campaign on the environment, health-care, and training. Possibly also Company profitability, but let's focus on the first three just now.

Okay, let me just. Now. The first thing is to find Board members connected to outside companies that could bid for the new subsidies and, naturally, get them. If such companies don't already exist, we need to find people who will set them up in order to receive the subsidies and who will, in the meantime, donate to your campaign. As I said, Fraser, *I am your bridge.*

Yes, well, just doing my job. So, you'll be glad to know, I have some ideas already. I'll schedule some meetings for next week, if that's all right. It might be a plan for you to give me access to your webDisk. That way I can schedule appointments with donors directly into your diary, without having to call and check with you every time. Okay? Great.

No, all I need's the password. Just jot it down here.

Certain Board members, I happen to know, are very impressed with you already. They trust you. Trust, Fraser, is a rare and important commodity in corporate politics. If you can maintain the Board members' trust, then you can get re-selected as often as you like. Get too big for your boots, though, and it's bye-bye time. If and when you get selected, you must always remember what put you there. It's not the employee electors - <u>dumb cunts vote for whoever throws the biggest promotional budget at them</u> - it's not even the Board - it's the promotional budget itself. The donors. Never forget that. And never forget that they're the ones who are keeping you there. You piss them off, Fraser, and don't think they won't come down on you like a ton of bricks. Newspaper-sized bricks. The stories you start seeing about yourself, they won't be pretty. We all know who owns the papers, TV, and pretty much most of the internet that anyone who washes often enough to actually work here uses. Piss off the donors, and in the space of three months they'll have every single employee clamouring for your resignation. But they'd rather not go down that road, Fraser. They'd far rather back a man they can trust. A man like you.

As I was. As. If you honour that trust, if you honour it Fraser, you can expect a golden handshake that will more than make up for the relatively crappy financial package that comes with the job. Non-executive director-ships on the boards of all the other companies; public speak-ing engagements at all their foundations. You'll get half a million just for blowing your nose on a podium. So you can think of the Directorship of United Solutions as a cheap key, pretty mean-looking in itself, which nevertheless opens the door to a bank vault. Don't throw away that key before you've unlocked the door, Fraser! Think of Mr Kinnaird mak-ing speeches for the Flag Group, and making, what, ten times his old salary in the process. Just from speeches. Which is something you're good at anyway. Did you study that, did you, public speaking? Did you pay a trainer?

Well, lucky you.

If you say so. No, I mean I know so, of course. Yes.

Oh, you are. And not only that, you're also a man who

the *employees think* they can trust. You've got it going on, Fraser. You're warm, approachable, down-to-earth. A nice modern family man who everyone would love to have as a next door neighbour. Hell, Fraser, *I'd* love to have you as a next door neighbour.

Oh yes. Sure. So. I think that's us all done now. I'll schedule these meetings into your diary for next week.

I beg your pardon?

I beg your pardon, Fraser?

How the hell would that work? The entire point –

No, no you're quite wrong there, Fraser. Donations don't interfere with the Employee Choice principle, they *uphold* it. If we were to give all the candidates money from the central purse to fund their campaigns, then that would mean the employees having to - indirectly - fund candidates they haven't voted for, and whose views they may, in fact, oppose! That's not fair now, is it? We went over this at the beginning.

And how, exactly, could you do that? How could you run election campaigns on no money whatsoever?

The internet is not the answer to everything, Fraser. You can't just put manifestos on websites and expect people to *read* them. I can tell you – I might take this opportunity to remind you - the donors control the media that all our employees happen to choose to read. Want to read. If you try and rock the boat, you can kiss bye-bye to your career, because every employee will be reading about your failures in their lunchtime sandwich of Jennifers Aniston and Lopez. <u>You have no idea just how gullible these people are! You have to understand, they don't actually want to think. What they want, is to be *told* what to think.</u> Trust me, okay. I've been in this game a long time, Mr McDowell, a very long time.

Well. I'm telling you - they can turn on you in a matter of hours, fed the right stories. It would make me sad to see that happen to you, Fraser, because I think you have a real gift. You shouldn't squander a gift like that. It would be a terrible waste, if you were to ruin yourself. Like Robert King.

Well, the *funny* thing is, he had an idea along the same lines as yours. To make all election campaigns cost-free. Cut out the donors. Rather a coincidence - for two highly intelligent men, to come up with exactly the same impractical scheme. You can't have heard about it, I suppose?

Mm.

Yes, exactly the same.

It was so sad, so *sordid,* all those stories that came out about him. Three nursing students! In one night! In a *Travelodge*! What was the name of that one. Ice-cubes. In her mouth.

Mm, *doesn't* it? And yet, sixty million *intelligent* people can't be wrong, can they?

Ha! Right. So we're all clear, are we, Fraser? We're singing from the same hymn sheet?

Good, good. I'm looking forward to working with you. I think you've got what it takes. I think you're going to go all the way, I really do. It's going to be *exciting*, Fraser.

No. No, you're all right Fraser. I must admit you shook me a wee bit! But if you assure me. Yes. Well, that's what they love you for! A bit of that 'blue sky' thinking! Just a bit, eh. Just a bit.

Yes. Splendid.

No problem, Fraser. Any time you want something - any time you need - I'm only a phone call away. And sometimes I'm even nearer than that. Ha ha!

*Absolutely.*

Bye.

He's away, Henry. Did you get it all?

Hello? Is this thing working?

Henry?

Don't tell me it's fucking broken.

I wanted to get that racist joke on tape.

Hello? Henry?

Hello?

# SUICIDE OF UNITED SOLUTIONS ADVISER IN INSIDER TRADING SCANDAL

31.07.10

by Sherina Marzam

A senior adviser at corporate giant United Solutions has become the latest casualty of the collapse of Luker-Harding. Henry Pusanto had invested heavily in the company shortly before it was revealed to have used misleading accounting techniques. His body was discovered by his daughter Ellen inside his car this morning, in the family garage. He is believed to have died from car exhaust asphyxiation. Further medical details have yet to be publicly confirmed.

Luker-Harding's practice of hiding risk in off-balance sheet accounts precisely echoes the events that triggered the current financial crisis. Many of the most spectacular collapses at the start of the Credit Crunch were exacerbated by the extra operating room allowed by such veiled accounting procedures. Investors may have supposed that such practices were now high on auditors' watch lists.

But Luker-Harding convinced auditors that its circumstances were unique. Because its subsidiary companies specialised in meeting guaranteed supply contracts for United Solutions, it was seen to be a 'safe bet'. The share price rose further after the appointment of new CEO John Hampsteed last month. According to a respected source, Pusanto made his investment shortly before the appointment was announced. The revelation comes at a crucial time for Fraser McDowell, the new director of United Solutions, and his mission to root out sleaze.

It is of course no secret that Hampsteed enjoys a cordial friendship with Mr McDowell. The two were contemporaries at university and have remained close since, sharing a very public vision for 'ethical capitalism'. The fact that Hampsteed is clearly the sort of man with whom McDowell would like to see United do more business, in conjunction with his proven management expertise, meant that his acceptance of the post gave the share price a substantial fillip. If Luker-Harding had been seen as a safe bet before Hampsteed's appointment, many believed that it was now a copper-bottomed one. This newspaper was not alone in expressing such a belief at the time of the appointment.

However, Hampsteed shocked investors by revealing the true state of the company's accounts last week. His uncompromising stance mirrors McDowell's own. Mr McDowell is known to have been impressed by Hampsteed's openness and honesty at Luker-Harding's shareholder meeting. 'It takes true courage and leadership to give people the unpalatable truth, instead of sugared falsehoods,' he said at the time. The same could also apply to his own courageous approach since taking the helm at United: he is very much seen as a new broom.

Speaking to this newspaper after we confronted him over Pusanto's suicide and share dealing, Mr McDowell said, 'The timing of Henry's share purchases does seem to indicate involvement in some kind of insider trading. Obviously his activities backfired, with tragic consequences.' He went on to speak about the importance of eradicating insider trading from his corporation, whose core brand values have always been openness, honesty and fairness. He called for an end to 'the get-rich-quick culture and all its dangerous temptations - dangers not just for individuals like Henry, but for the long-term health of business and society as a whole.'

Luker-Harding is widely expected to be bought by the Flag Group in a rescue package to be worked out in conjunction with United Solutions, but Mr McDowell refused to comment on this. Given Mr McDowell's public admiration for Hampsteed, however, it is widely believed that Hampsteed will remain in his role as CEO - this time at the head of a business with clean books. When asked whether he thought Hampsteed had given Luker-Harding's shareholders a fair deal in wiping millions off the value of the company with his revelations, Mr McDowell replied, 'We have to look beyond short-term gain and focus on long-term financial health, which is what John Hampsteed is quite rightly trying to do. This approach will be much more sustainable, much better for everyone, including the shareholders of the future.'

Shares in the Flag Group have already risen 4.2% since purchase talks began for Luker-Harding, and are expected to rise further, so there is certainly at least one silver lining for investors.

## Marginalia

## Colette Paul

---

Surinder woke late, glad to have slept through the worst of the dark Saturday morning. It was ten o'clock. She lay and listened to the muffled traffic go up and down the street, children playing in the back greens behind her window. She'd been here five months, and had never been so alone. At home there had always been people around—her mother and father and sisters, her grandfather, the cook, the housekeeper—so much noise that she used to yearn for some peace and quiet. It wasn't the same, talking to people here. She had to concentrate on the accent, and the effort was tiring. She leant in too close to people, as if this would help close the disconnection between the hearing and the understanding of a word. A few weeks ago a girl at university had said, Surinder, some space, you're nearly on top of me, and although she knew it was meant in a good natured way, she'd become self conscious about initiating conversation. The anxiety had even leaked into her dreams, dreams where she opened her mouth to speak but nothing came out, or what came out was garbled; Punjabi and English muddled together.

She looked at the clock again and worked out what time it'd be at home, imagining each of her sisters in turn, and what they'd be doing. When she got bored of that, she got up quickly, shivering with the cold, and put on her dressing-gown over the pyjamas and sweatshirt she wore to bed. A few days ago her flatmate, Kirsten, had gone home for Christmas, so she had the place to herself. Even though Kirsten spent a lot of time at her boyfriend's house or in her room with the door shut, it felt oddly quiet without her. It was the university holidays and she'd no classes, nothing to do. Yesterday morning she'd brought her all text books into the living room, thinking she'd make a start on her dissertation. She'd organized her stationary and notes and pads over the table by the window. But instead of starting, she'd spent the afternoon watching telly, flicking through old Hello! magazines Kirsten had left. Then she'd cleaned the kitchen, and went out for some shopping. By the time she got home, it had begun to snow. She'd leant out of the window and watched it drift soundlessly out of the black sky, like a magic trick, disappearing as soon as it hit the ground. She felt like laughing with the wonderment of it, that here she was, seeing with her own eyes something she'd only read about in books. She reached out and let the last, slow snowflakes fall on her hand. It was hard to imagine that it was not snowing over the whole universe, but only her part of it—that at home her family would be asleep, the house locked up for the night, the dogs barking in the yard.

She'd felt restless the rest of the evening, and had started to write a letter to her friend from home, trying to describe it all. He hadn't gone to university: he was working in his father's office, typing invoices. His letters were full of what he'd been reading and thinking about. It's true what Marx said, he'd write, religion is the opium of the people; despair is the only viable position, if you really have your eyes open in the world. Surinder spent a long time over her letters back, although she was careful that the final version was messy and off-hand, full of doodles and scribbled out words, like his. (Excuse the marginalia, she had written in one, knowing Sanjit would be pleased by the word—that was the kind of person he was). They had kissed, once, a few months before she left. The next day he'd met her on the street to tell her he didn't think of her in that way, he supposed she was the closest thing he had to a friend and he hoped this wouldn't spoil things. Surinder said no, not at all. No, of course not. When she wrote the letters, the pain of that day would come back to her. She was careful to imply her full and exciting life, saying she didn't think she could ever go back to

India, India was on its last legs: he wrote back to tell her he was jealous. Sometimes she wrote long, gloomy passages about being depressed by the state of the world, but these felt as theatrical and untrue as her portrayal of herself as a social butterfly. In truth she experienced, almost daily, bursts of elation followed by bursts of utter desolation, and both scared her in a way she could not explain.

The living room was painted dark red, with white borders. It was dark and damp and musty-smelling. There was an old marble fireplace, with an electric fire that didn't work, and two stained brown velvet couches. Neither of them sat here much. Once, just after Surinder had moved in, she'd cooked a meal for them, and they'd had a nice night, sitting at the table. Kirsten had told her about the trouble she was having with her boyfriend. He was only twenty six, a few years older than Kirsten, but already had a little girl from a previous relationship. The little girl's mother made things difficult for them, always calling him up late at night, changing plans without notice. Also, he got depressed; he was a very deep person, Kirsten said. Surinder had nodded sympathetically, judiciously, flattered by such confidences. Kirsten asked her about arranged marriages, if Surinder would have an arranged marriage, and Surinder said no, her parents weren't traditional like that. In fact it was her mother who'd pushed her to apply for the scholarship, who had urged her to take the place at Glasgow when the letter arrived. Kirsten said her boyfriend was very clever, cleverer than her, but he kept failing his exams; his nerves got the better of him. She asked Surinder if he seemed a nervous person to her.

Surinder, who'd only met him a few times, said no, not really. Kirsten perked up, and said that was because she didn't know him. Towards the end of the night, she mentioned places they should go to together, certain bars she liked, an authentic Indian restaurant that only a few people knew about, but nothing had come of it. As the weeks had gone on they'd become friendly, but not friends. It was the same with the other students in the University, and Surinder had to remind herself that these things take a long time. At night she would lie in bed, thinking out her plans. She liked to set herself goals every week, even if it was just going to the cinema, or taking a book to read over coffee at the Costa café on campus. On Sundays, when she spoke to her mum, she always had something to tell her. It was for her mother's sake she'd accepted an invitation to go for dinner tonight at the Singh's, the son of her father's old school friend. She had never met them before. On the phone he'd sounded formal and bored. He was Glaswegian, but his wife was from the Punjab, and he said she would enjoy talking about home with her. He'd given her complicated directions on how to get there, two buses then a fifteen minute walk, which she'd written down carefully, already feeling dread at the prospect of the whole thing. She'd spent all week trying not to worry about it.

The mail had come early today, and there were four birthday cards from home on the mat, waiting for her. To-morrow she would be twenty one. She studied the handwriting, then propped them behind the clock on the mantelpiece. There'd be nothing to look forward to if she opened them today. Her eyes kept wandering back to them, and she opened the curtains for distraction. It was a wide street, lined on both sides with rickety, dirty-looking shops—fruit stalls and two hardware shops, a discount chemist, a butchers, a café. When she moved in, Kirsten had mentioned that she'd feel at home here, that there was a big Asian community. Surinder had been offended. The people here were mostly Pakistani and Muslim, dark-skinned, not like her at all. The women went around in groups, or with children, and many of them wore the burka. In a strange way it made you think more about the body underneath, about hair and sweat and rolls of flesh. Surinder wore jeans and jumpers, her long hair plaited down her back, and was not like them at all. It was odd to think that people here lumped them all together. Once, when she'd been slow packing her bags in the supermarket, an old woman behind her had said, loudly, They expect everyone to wait for them, but she'd pretended not to hear. It was nothing to get upset about.

She ate some yogurt and a banana, then had a long shower. The phone went just as she was getting out, but it was someone looking for Kirsten. She wrote their name down carefully on the pad, under the names of other people who had called for her. Kirsten was always busy, always out and about. Sometimes a few of her girlfriends came over and they'd spend the evening in the living room, drinking wine. Often, before she left for a night out, she'd tell Surinder that she didn't want to go, that she wished she could stay at home. 'I'm stressed out,' she'd say. Surinder had taken to repeating this phrase at Uni, just as she would say, if anyone asked her, that she'd spent the weekend chilled out. In fact, weekends were her loneliest time, and she was always glad when they were over.

She looked through her wardrobe, wondering what to wear to dinner. She'd brought two saris with her, one red and one purple, but she would feel conspicuous, riding the bus in them. It was raining and she'd have to wear her boots and coat and scarf over the top. She decided instead on a pair of black trousers and a red shirt she'd bought recently, taking them out the wardrobe and hanging them over her chair. It was two o'clock now: three more hours to fill. She made a cup of tea and wandered idly round the flat. She stood outside Kirsten's door, then pushed it open slightly. She stood for a second, as if waiting for someone to stop her, then went inside. The heavy green velvet curtains were still drawn so it was quite dark. The bed was unmade, and there were clothes lying in heaps on the floor, two pint glasses full of old water on the bedside table. Kirsten herself looked slightly dirty but glamorous, as if she hadn't had time to wash her hair or face for a while. She wore heavy eye makeup, and tight black jeans. One of her favourite t-shirts, the Frankie says RELAX one, was thrown over the bedpost. An entire wall next to the bed was covered with photographs. Some of them looked like family snaps, and others were obviously taken on nights out with her friends. A lot of them were of her boyfriend, alone or with her. He had curly black hair and pale, rosy skin. Unlike Kirsten, he looked incredibly clean. Once Surinder had come into the sitting room in the morning to find him sitting in his boxer shorts, watching telly. His legs and chest were covered in furls of black hair. He wasn't embarrassed, and had begun to chat, asking her how she found Glasgow and telling her about the band he was in. A few weeks later, Surinder had seen him talking intently to a girl in a café on Byres Road, holding her hand across the table. It hadn't crossed her mind to tell Kirsten, but she felt awkward whenever she mentioned his name. Once or twice she'd heard her crying after speaking to him on the phone, but the next day everything would seem fine again. 'That's us back on,' Kirsten would say, full of the joys.

She sat on the bed and tried to imagine what it would be like having Kirsten's life. Quickly she took off her sweatshirt and put on the Frankie t-shirt. Then she took off her baggy jeans, and put on a pair of black leggings lying on the floor. She went over to the mirror and looked at herself. There was a red lipstick lying on its side with the top off, and she put that on as well. She walked around the room, trying to get a feel for it. She examined the CDs, and looked through a book called Feel the Fear and Do It Anyway. She was deciding what answers she would give to the quiz—how confident are you?—when she heard footsteps on the landing. She sat still, her heart pounding. But they passed down the stairs. The fright was enough to make her change quickly, putting everything back. She closed the door tightly, and went into her own room. She lay on her bed with her eyes closed, listening to the rain fall into the darkening street. She thought of Sanjit, then of Kirsten's boyfriend, and then they both fell away and she was left only with a vague hunger for something, anything, to happen to her. She fell asleep for an hour, and woke with a fright. It was half five, and she had to be in Dennistoun for seven.

The first bus took her into Shawlands. She'd been told to get off at the public toilets, next to the park, and get a number thirty-eight. The streets were full of shoppers making their way home, the traffic packed solid down the street. She looked in a shop window at a display of push-up bras,

covering the Mr Kipling French Fancies she'd bought with
her umbrella. Now that she was out, part of the crowd, she
felt quite light-hearted. It was good having something to do
on a Saturday night. There would probably be lots of home-
cooked food, and her mouth watered at the thought of aloo
gobi, dhal, butter chicken, chicken tikka, piles of hot roti.
Whatever happened, it would be an experience, and that was
the most important thing. Even at this moment, standing in
a street she didn't know, getting two buses to an area she
didn't know, watching a drunk man wave his can at passers-
by: it was all an experience.

   The thirty-eight was busy, and she had to stand, holding onto the bar, as it lurched through the streets. After a
while the shops emptied out, and they were travelling down
a straight black motorway, the distance hollowed out in
darkness. She began to worry about missing her stop, and
was relieved when the ESSO garage appeared. She got off
two stops later. She'd to turn right and walk until she came
to a roundabout, then turn left. The street was deserted, the
houses set far back and fenced with walls or gates. She was
already late, and walked quickly, her feet wet. The houses in
Elmtree Road were smaller, and sat in a squat grey row that
snaked onto the distance. When she reached number sixteen, all the windows were dark, the driveway empty. She
rang the bell, smoothing down her hair, and waited. No answer. She rang again. She got the directions out of her
pocket and double checked the address. After a while she
looked through the letter box, but it was dark and she
couldn't see anything. She didn't know what to do. What if
they'd just popped out for five minutes; if she left now they'd
think she hadn't bothered to turn up at all. She was peering
up and down the street when a woman came out of next
door, calling, 'Hello hello, are you looking for the Singhs?'

   Surinder nodded, walking over, and the woman told
her they'd had to take the little one to the hospital. He'd been
running a temperature and the doctor told them to go to the
Southern General in case it was meningitis. She said they'd
asked her to keep an eye out for Surinder, to let her know;

they'd tried to call, but she must have already left the house.

Surinder walked back down the street. She was surprised by how disappointed, and how miserable, she felt. It was raining heavily now, and it was getting into her boots, running down her neck. She thought of the whole week stretching ahead of her, the flat freezing cold, everything shut for Christmas.

At least the bus came quickly; she sat beside the window, leaning her head against the glass. There were a handful of stars in the sky, but no moon. After a while, she opened the box of French Fancies and polished three off in one go. A stream of people got on and off. An old woman plonked down beside her, shaking water from her coat.

'Oh Lordy,' she said, 'what's this weather like? I bet you don't have this where you come from.' Surinder smiled and the woman said, 'Sorry hen, am I crushing you here?'

'No, I'm alright,' said Surinder.

The box of cakes was still open on her lap, and she thought maybe it'd be polite to offer the woman one. She chose the chocolate flavour. She told Surinder she'd been visiting her sister who had emphysema—'Never smoke hen,' she said, 'not that I can talk, I'm at it like a chimney'—and they'd had a wee drink, it was Christmas after all. She asked if her people were allowed to drink, and Surinder said yes, her dad liked whisky. The woman said she liked a whisky herself, or a Baileys, sometimes a wee Bacardi & Coke. She said her man had died last year so she was just going to have a quiet Christmas, and then she told her about her husband's illness. He was completely blind at the end up. People didn't know how to deal with it; they'd cross the street to avoid them.

'Why did they do that?' Surinder said.

'Because they're ignorant bastards,' the woman said, her cheeks trembling. Her skin was shiny and liver-coloured from the cold: she didn't look well herself.

The bus had been sitting at the stop for a while, and now the driver came out the cab and said he'd broken down, they were sending a replacement. They were in the middle of

the Gorbals, high-rise flats on one side, derelict waste
ground full of torn billboards on the other. The old woman
said she might as well walk from here—she pointed to one of
the tower blocks and said, 'That's me there.' There was only
one other man waiting for the replacement bus, and he was
swearing under his breath, his face screwed up. He'd been
smoking at the back of the bus, and when the driver asked
him to put it out, he'd ignored him. Surinder didn't fancy
waiting with him, and said she was going to walk too. The
old woman said it wasn't a nice part of town to be walking by
herself, she'd chum her to the newsagents. Everyone knew
her round here, they'd leave her alone. Even though she was
relieved Surinder said oh, no, she didn't have to do that, and
the woman said she'd worry otherwise. Anyway, she said,
she needed to work off some of this lard. She walked slowly,
rocking from side to side, breathless. Surinder had to slow
down to match her. It was raining again, puddles collecting
in the dips of the street. She asked Surinder what she was
studying, and if she liked it. She said her mum must be
proud of her. Surinder said there were things she liked about
Glasgow, and things she missed from home. She missed her
family and friends. When she said it out loud she felt suddenly sorry for herself for she realized, at that moment, that
she hated it here and that it was never going to get any better, even when she was older.

    The feeling stayed with her as they said goodbye. The
woman turned back the way they'd come and she walked on,
past the job centre, past the yard that sold gravestones, past
the new flats at the top of Victoria Road, thin lines of light
shining from behind the curtains. It was unbelievable to
think that all the people who lived there must consider their
lives as important and singular as she considered hers. The
rain hit off the car roofs, making a lonely sound. A group of
boys appeared on the opposite side of the road, shouting and
pushing at each other, and because she was scared of them,
she forced herself not to speed up. When they passed, she
began to run. It'd been a long time since she'd run, and it felt
good, the muscles in her legs stretching, her arms swinging

back and forth. There was no one to see her and she didn't care even if there was. The rain fell down her face, splashed onto her trousers. She thought about being twenty one tomorrow, repeating the number to herself, how old it was, remembering when she'd been young. She felt tender for her young self. She kept running, thinking that at twenty one most famous people hadn't done anything yet—everything was still ahead of her, she could do anything she wanted to. All she had to do was set her mind to it. And everything, really, was alright. Everything was alright. And even if it wasn't—even if no boys ever fell in love with her, even if everyone ignored her and laughed at her and despised her (which they didn't) then that'd be okay too. They could go ahead. Because she was twenty one tomorrow, and strong, and everything was ahead of her.

# The End

## Allan Wilson

---

**FLASH**

We dance.

**FLASH FLASH FLASH FLASH FLASH FLASH**

We turn into trance strings.

We swoop
over
    each
      other.
        Veryveryveryveryvery fast.

We're the breath in the air. We're the clack of a stiletto heel. We're family. There's faces we recognise and faces we don't but we're all the same and we will be. Forever. We all clap. And we all cheer. And we all sing

**HERE WE, HERE WE, HERE WE FUCKING GO**

Arms on shoulders, sharing sweat

**HERE WE, HERE WE, HERE WE FUCKING GO**

Outside. The street. It's different here. Colder. The five of us line the pavement from the tarmac to the takeaway. Nothing remains but tonight. And nothing should. None of us have ever been this happy and we will never be again. Nobody has died here and nobody will ever fucking die in this world. Not in this fucking world we've created. Not now. Not again.

*Oh will we jump into the canal and swim across it?*
*I'll jump in if you jump in.*
*Take ma hand and help me into the water.*
*Then you help me in. Ok Simon?*
*Aye, that's ok.*
*I used both ma arms to lower him down. Oh it's cold.*
*Oh it's freezing cold, he said.*
*Do you want me to pull you out?*
*No no no. It's cold but it's ok. It's like the swimming*
*baths when you first go in.*
*Is it not dirty but?*
*It isny dirty. It's water. Water is clean.*
*Aye, but it's brown.*
*Och, that's ok. Just come in and you'll see. It's cold but*
*it's nice.*

Pain doesn't exist. Hate doesn't exist. Our Mums don't even exist. We exist: Jamie, Steiny, Davie, Dylan, and Me. The masters of the Universe. We are Rangers, Super Rangers. We are the Staffy Primary Seven Football Team. But we're missing Simon that's gone away. Simonthatsgoneaway. Right after primary seven.

But it's survival of the fittest so

Most of the time I forget his face. I forget his smell and his laugh. One day I'll forget his name. First his second name and then finally his first.
Is somebody's Da pickin us up?
I'm pickin up your Maw Steiny, says Davie.
Here Steiny, is it not your Da that's gettin us? I say.
Nah, it was my Da two weeks ago. It's your Da this week.

Nah, my Da says he's never gettin us again. He doesn't want to get stopped with four in the back again case he loses his license.

Poof, says Davie.

Your Da's a what? I say.

Asphinctersayswhat, says Dylan.

Aye, your Maw's a sphincter, says Steiny.

What's a fuckin sphincter anyway? Davie says.

Jamie points at him and we all look. Here, see that thing that stares back at you when you look in your Maw's mirror, that's a sphincter.

What, ma face? he says.

Naw, your fanny, ya fanny! Jamie says.

Everybody laughs. Then Jamie stops us.

We better be getting picked up. It's fucking freezing, he says.

And we all begin to realise it is. Our shirts are stuck to us and clinging to our chests. The sweat on our heads pins our hair to our scalps.

*Oh I'll tan you, he said. I'll tan you cos I'm faster.*
*I'll beat you more like, I said.*
*Hahaha shoosh. I'm fastest in the school.*
*Should we take off our shoes? Will it make us faster?*
*If we keep them on we'll both be slower and it'll be equal.*
*Oh I'm going to tan you wee man, he said.*
*You're a faster runner but I might be a faster swimmer.*

Swear to fuck guys. My Da's not coming.

Fuck sake.

Seriously?

Aye seriously, I say.

Now Adam, says Steiny, is your Da a gypsy?

We can walk, I say.

Have you got a gypsy Da Adam? Have you? Is he a hairy gypsy?

You can fuckin walk. We'll get a taxi, Jamie says.

I've got no fuckin cash left man, says Dylan.

I'm not walking myself.

His Da's definitely a gypsy. I always suspected. Steiny
nods around the boys.

It was your fuckin turn to give us a lift, Jamie says

Shut your teeth, Steiny. Jamie you can fuck off too.

And now it's just me and Jamie looking at each other.

You're always so fuckin unorganised, he says

And your Da is Gypsy Rose Lee, Steiny sings.

It's not ma fuckin turn, I say. It's fuckin Steiny's turn
or yours.

Jamie, leave it man. Think about it eh? Now's not the
time, Dylan says.

Jamie shakes his head. Laughs. When's it ever the
time with him, fuck sake. He steps towards me and knocks
me with his shoulder. Right, if anybody's wantin a taxi then
come with me. He looks me up and down. Or you can stay wi
bawbag here.

Jamie walks up the street. Steiny and Davie follow.
Dylan stays beside me. Steiny's giving it, here look, look, my
crystal ball is saying that yes, Adam really is a bawbag.
Davie's laughing and nodding his head like a puppy. Jamie's
growling at me. He won't look away. I lower my eyes.

*I sat on the canal bank. There was long grass and*
*bushes of stingy nettles between me and the canal.*
*Simon was kicking his legs and grabbing onto the*
*grass. Sometimes the water splashed up and it got into*
*his mouth and he spat.*
*Are you ok Simon?*
*Aye Adam. Now you come down. It's fun.*

Jamie's bein a bawchew, says Dylan.

Fuck off mate, I say.

Here, it wasn't me who said your Da was a gypsy!

Dylan gonnae just get tae fuck man!

Naw. I won't. Plus I owe that prick a tenner. He'll try
and make me pay the taxi.

Thought you had no cash?

He waggles his shoe at me. It jingles. Always got the emergency fund, he says.

Dylan's shite always makes me laugh.

My Da's not a gypsy you know, I say.

He nods, smirks.

He's fuckin not!

Aye, I know. I know.

I turn away from Dylan and look at the traffic. I feel a presence beside me in the amber light of the street lamps and the glint of headlights that reflects off the puddles. I turn to the movements. I start to speak but no words come out when I see them open the taxi door.

The taxi speeds off and I batter its windows as hard as I can as it pulls out. I scuff the windows with the palm of my hand. Two of their faces peer out the back window of the hack. I can't tell which ones. All I can see is their middle fingers erect and the taxi fades away as I run out on to the road to chase them down and

*We were holding onto each other and kicking. We were coughing when water splashed us. We were laughing very loud.*

We see girls from our year. Every week they go to the unders then come out and hit the overs. Kirstie is there and I know the drill. They leave the club and go up a lane. One of them will wallop a bottle of vodka out of her wee clutch bag and the four girls will whoop and whistle as they pass it between each other. They'll talk about the boys they kissed and fondled and got fingered by

like a fuckin baby's arm!

And the vodka will swill around them all.

Here, I'm gonna boke!

Well do it beside a bin then ya fud.

Dylan and I nod to each other and follow them. We step further into the dark and watch them.

Kirstie sways from the circle to the side of the lane and

chunks scrape from her gut onto the iron bin side. The splashback licks at her bare feet, her toes covered in brown snowdrops, rancid voddy cokes, and she retches again, harder. When it stops she falls back into the group. They huddle close together and spark up fags.

Shoulda brought a jacket.

Fuck that.

Aye, fuck that.

It's heavy baltic but, brass monkeys.

Here, drink up.

The bottle is passed and after a sook at her fag Kirstie swigs in the booze.

A wee bit down the lane is a parked car and she goes to it. Swaggering, Beyoncelike, like a cat prowling. The mirror is fogged up but she wipes it with the back of her hand and drops of condensation drip from her skin. She looks at herself. Pouts. She fumbles about in her purse and brings out a tub of lip balm. It's in a metal case and she clicks the lid open. The balm rubs on her lips and she moulds them together for a second then pops them open. Her lips dazzle and sparkle like icicles. She kisses the mirror and leaves a greasy smear on the glass.

The bottle is nearly empty now.

You look like you've just been shafted! says big Lynne.

I feel like it. My belly. Rockin like fuck so it was.

Rockin like ye had a cock in ye mean.

Aye. Here gies some eh that vodka.

It's passed to Kirstie who takes a glug. She throws it back like it's diluting juice. The other girls look at her and she goes to boke again. They step back. Her speckled brown feet wobble. You can almost see the sick in her stomach move up the pipe and through her throat. Just where her make-up line meets her skin, just at the top of her neck, it's as if it's bulging. Her cheeks swell. And then subside. Everything happens in reverse now. The colour returns to her face and the group all step together like they're being danced in.

I swallowed a wee bit of ma own sick there, she says.

Big Lynne raises a diva hand.

Your breath, darlin, will be manky, she says.

Aw I don't like it. Don't like it. The taste of the sick is gonna make me sick. Here, gies some eh that coke.

Eh, nut! Don't want your chunder in it!

Aw God, it tastes like death Lynne! Aw hurry, gie me the coke.

Here, fuck sake. She hands it to Kirstie. Kirstie drinks a few mouthfuls, screws up her face then burps a beast. She hands the bottle back to Lynne.

Doll, dae you really expect me to drink this now? she says, then launches the remains up the lane.

Lynne links arms with Kirstie and they walk back towards the club. That's when they see us in the doorway.

Awright boys, says big Lynne, what yous doin in there? Shaggin?

Gonna gie us a wee swig eh that vodka darlin, says Dylan.

The girls crowd around the doorway.

Eh and whit vodka's that then? says big Lynne, her arms folded across her chest.

Dylan looks to me, nods to her bag and coughs.

It's just we thought you had vodka in your bag there Lynne, I say.

You no a bit too young tae drink wee man, she says. Maybe wait until your baws drop?

All the girls laugh except Kirstie. She's swaying a wee bit and screwing her eyes up as she looks at us like she's not quite sure if we're really happening. For a second it looks like she's reaching into her bag for ID.

So are you ladies planning tae go tae the overs? Dylan says, loosening an extra shirt button.

The girls laugh again and turn to big Lynne. A sneaky grin spreads across her face. She whispers something to each of them in turn. They giggle. Emma looks us up and down. Kirstie sways. They link their arms into ours and drag us along.

*I was clinging onto the canal bank and his legs and*

*arms were splashing. His head slipped under the water and then came out further up. The rain was hitting off the water so hard then that the drops sprayed back up and all the splashes looked like big scuttling spiders.*

The same bouncers they were chatting to before are manning the doors. They smirk at the girls and wink. Then a hand presses my chest and his voice says "not tonight boys." The girls are halfway inside as we give them a final glance then slink away. But big Lynne comes out, the experience of every single one of her sixteen years backing us up.

Eh, scuse me? I think you'll find they're wi me. Diva hands right in their faces.

I don't care who they're wi. They're no getting in.

And why's that then? Why's that?

Cos whit age are they?

Whit age are they? Whit age are they? They're twenty five is what age they are.

Me and Dylan just look at each other. I don't know if he's about to laugh or greet.

Aye very good hen. Say goodnight tae yer boyfriends and you'll see them in school the morra.

Whit are you tryin tae say they're no? Cos if that's the case then I'd like tae see the manager. And see while I'm telling him about this I'm also gonnae tell him about how every week yous two try and take wee lassies. Wee. Lassies. Fourteen, fifteen year old, oot the back tae try and get your hole.

Now wait a wee minute here, the guy says.

Lynne stops him with a wagging finger.

And I'll tell ye what else doll. See speed dial seven in ma phone, straight through tae the News of the World. And I'm sure they'll be interested in the stories I've got tae tell about this place and yous two.

The two bouncers look at each other. Dylan and me look at each other. We look at the bouncers. Then everyone turns back to Lynne.

And ma Da says if I get any trouble wae fannies like

you then I've tae call him and he'll be round in two minutes
flat. Is that whit ye want? Ye want tae fight ma da?

One of the bouncers turns to the other and says, look
twenty five tae you?

Bouncer goes, aye. In ye go gents, have a good night.

They step aside for me and Dylan to enter. Following
up the rear is big Lynne. We turn to her, smile, then it's

Jackets in a corner. Tunes pumping. They're dancing.
We're watching. Kirstie slops out of their handbag circle,
slips by Dylan and me. There's a glimmer of recognition as
she looks at me a second too long. Then she's gone and the
bathroom door swings shut behind her. I hear heavy breathing in the gaps between beats.

Fuck it, says Dylan.

I watch him tilt his head from side to side then march
to the middle of the dance floor. He reaches the circle of girls
and looks at each face in turn. He stops. He taps at Lynne's
shoulder and she turns around. I wish I could hear what he
whispers in her ear. Whatever it is her face softens and she
nods along as he speaks.

I turn and stare at the bathroom door. It opens both
ways as girls come and go. Soon I begin to see the same
faces with brighter eyes and redder lips. Kirstie never leaves.
I could go to the girls on the dance floor and ask for help. I'll
lose eye contact with the door. The door is wooden and
heavy. There's a stick figure girl carved in red plastic. When
girls come and go I see slivers of light in the gaps. There are
sinks against both walls. A row of mirrors above the sinks.
They reflect the room upon itself so it is endless.

I move closer and as the door swings shut I bar it with
my foot. I try to peer under cubicle doors. The floor glimmers
with water and sweat. I kneel down to get a better view and I
don't feel it coming. A hand grips my shoulder and twists my
arm up behind my back. His voice tells me that my night is
over. He sounds as if he's laughing while he pushes me so
fast that I stumble. I ask him to stop. To wait just a fucking
minute. To wait just a fucking minute please. It's not time

for me to go yet. It's not my time to go. We pass Dylan and big Lynne. I call out. They're entwined in each other, saliva lashing at each other's tongues.

The music still pumps. The lights still flash. Between beats my calls are unheard. The last thing I see is a slice of light from the swinging door. In the light I see the edge of a mirror. In the mirror there are a million faces that could be her or me or memories of anyone and

The street is empty now. The doors of the club are shut tight. There are scuff marks down the red paint and I know I won't succeed where others have failed. I bury my hands into my pockets, lean against a wall. The doorway reeks of piss.

Later she comes out in the same way as me. She seems limp in the bouncer's arms. He places her down on the pavement and her bare legs spasm and recoil as the dampness strikes them. She lifts her head to the bouncer and presses her palm against the cold grit as his hands leave her body. He grimaces, then shakes his head and smirks.

Kirstie sways a little, her voice a long tired drawl.

Aye, yer maw, she says.

---

My maw's dead, he says.

*Kick to stay above the water. I heard him laugh and it made me laugh. I laughed so hard that I couldn't breathe. Keep kicking, keep kicking. It was raining and it was getting dark. If we keep kicking we'll be ok. Froggy kick, remember. But I got scared. I turned back.*

I'm a stranger. To know someone for a fragment of time is nothing. When that time no longer exists there's only a memory, and maybe that doesn't exist either. Everything from the moment on is perception. We're strangers now. I could talk to her and perhaps she'd talk back. I could help her up and perhaps we'll walk off together and into the dark.

Her friends will be forgotten and mine will forget me. We can merge into the fog.

Soon this moment will be nothing more. It will not be written down. It will not be recorded. The same faces will walk the streets as night goes from darkness to light. The sun will rise behind clouds. People will do what they always do. From here to the end of the world my name will be forgotten even by those who were closest to me. I am the breath that gets stolen by the air. I am a shadow lost to the night. Kirstie spits up sick and it drips slowly out of her mouth. Dribbles of thick black liquid run down her chin and onto the bare skin above her cleavage. She giggles as she wipes her mouth with her arm. In the end there is no one to hold.

*All I heard was whistles. My eyes couldn't see him but I heard the whistles. I couldn't see his face. I couldn't hear his voice. I only heard him whistling. The rain vanished in the water. Then the whistling stopped. Then there was no sound.*

## The Malt Kiln

## Suhayl Saadi

Four walls, the darkness and Mark. A wall for each year, and every day weighed on her, like sand, like soil. Yet it was better to live in the grit of the earth and not to see the fractures. There were no mirrors in her flat. Frosted windows and beautiful prints. Sandpapered bath-taps. No mirrors. And here in The Kiln, everything was matt-black.

This'll help you dance, he said, though she wasn't sure how she managed to hear his voice over the music, as he placed something in her palm, a tiny blue flying-saucer emblazoned with the hologram of the head of a jester. The place swarmed with the unutterably slim. Laura held the joker close. She'd half-anticipated a degree of animation, but then she reminded herself that this was Hogmanay, New Year's Eve, and like everything to do with Eve, it was empty.

Mark's tongue darted in and out, and then he swallowed a handful. She resisted the temptation to smooth-down her flanks and instead let the music swirl around her: dark breaks of chemical beat mixed-in with longer phases of lounge core while every so often, a flash of speed garage would race through the retro-jungle ambience and emerge in a wadge of rampant, thumping house. Like the people, the music fluxed and yet stayed the same. But music had never been a slave. She closed her eyes, bit down on the face of the jester, and the beat was in her head.

The club was right on the river-bank and once had been a malt kiln, and after a while Laura found she was able to conjure up the two hundred year-old mathematics of its original structure as a dolphin might conjure up the architectures of the sea. The Kiln had a bell-tower which seemed to have been constructed of an older stone altogether and it was rumoured that before the kiln, on this site there had been a monastery.

Mark had disappeared. Her comptroller, her lover who regulated each glance and modulated every expression. With iron obedience, she'd orbited around him for so long, she'd almost forgotten what it had felt like, before, when the dark waters had been hers alone.

She looked around, and, though the house had turned deep and murky, she thought she saw him amongst a huddled group of skin dancers, yet she felt unsure of how long she'd had her eyes closed. The club had begun to sway, its star-shaped blackness swirled around in a freestyle mess. People had become mixed-up with objects and the stems of notes, with the dim, secreted lights that flashed in G minor from the walls, but now (and in the club, it was always now) she danced alone like everyone else. And yet, she found that touch and image did not align. That walls, tables, air, people, all held the same, fluctuating substance.

She could not see herself as she leapt and dived, yet she felt her skin roil and as though she were her own lover she began to enjoy the lean suppleness of her musculature, the fine touch of her banshee hair. The chamber was a stomach, a womb, and it disgorged, consumed and disgorged again and it was her womb, childless, motherless, bloodless. Or perhaps it was the empty, shrunken cavity of her own mother, the blazing schizo, whose lunacy now was compressed like celluloid into the jactance house, the bread of disgust which pumped from Laura's body. Phero-fucking-mone.

At certain points on the dance-floor, immersed in luminescent waterfalls, people momentarily would appear stark naked. The beams swept around, coalescing and fragmenting in a repetitive cycle, gathering up dancers as though they were bees. They would whirl on the spot, bodies glistening, hair swirling, nostrils flared. There was neither beginning nor end, everything was permissible.

Perhaps, thought Laura, it is the others who are deluded, the ones outside the beat, the fools who would hold hands and carry burning torches through this night. Sing songs, for auld lang syne, for Rabbie Burns, the randy farmer, lover of rodents and witches. But she had little need of this world. She had not eaten for days, it seemed. Sometimes, she would imagine becoming a self-sufficient being. A straight line, or possibly a dot.

But she was seeing spots, lines, zig-zags. *Fuck.* Laura spun at the fulcrum of the star with its seven corridors, each of which carried the dancers into carbon-black. She planted her soles wide and fixated on a table-leg, attempted to shut out everything else, intoned the words, *fat bitch, fat bitch, fat bitch.* Slowly, her vertigo began to settle and she was able to walk to the low table at which, carefully, she sat down.

After a time, she got up and allowed herself to re-join the flow. She was riding a river composed of perfectly-formed waves of blood and muscle. As she moved away from the main chamber, the music seemed to intensify, to become white noise and she had the impression that she was on all fours climbing like an insect up a wall. Suddenly, she felt a piece of cloth flap in her face. A whiff of old burning. Sacks of grain, perhaps, stored in this place during the interbellum. Or maybe it was the smell of Mark's semen, mingling with the sweat and scales of her skin. He was living, she was dead. Demand, feed, demand, feed. On good days, her breasts would leak.

Each of the aisles led to a self-contained chamber and in each of these, a different scene was being enacted. In one, the phantoms of old Glasgow comedians, of Murray, McGonigal, McLean and the Houston Sisters, mingled silently with the clubbers. In another, an imperial cohort charged perpetually at an unseen enemy; like words and time they could move in only one direction. In a third space, two men fought a perpetual duel, épées drawing silver arcs across the vault. As she ran past a fourth, Laura caught a glimpse of a woman, clad in a hooded shroud, standing on the brink of a great gulf. At her side was a small child. Following a momentary pause, woman and child together leapt over the edge.

The music had altered again, but she was uncertain as

to whether it was just another variation, or whether the antechamber which she was in was possessed of a different
sound altogether. She was sure that she could see the music
before her, and it was white and writhing, a monster of limbs
and mouths and a small, round head. The mouths gaped
and closed and the limbs constantly changed position like
those of a spider so that what at first had seemed to be a leg
now transformed into a long hand which proceeded desperately to clutch at the edges of one of the mouths, tugging at
it, working it furiously, only for the hand to change again
and become another thrashing leg. *The beast is pleasuring itself,* Laura said, aloud, *if at first you don't succeed, try, try
again,* though she did not hear her own words but rather,
saw them being anthropophagised. There was a mass of
brain behind the left ear. How had she managed to get away
from him, for this brief interlude? Was he really there, all
around, watching her from every crevice of this club, church,
kiln? *Mark, God of War. Get behind me!* She giggled.

And from the orifices of the beast, colours began to
pulse, to leap out and caress her and they found the crease
in her and flowed along its edges so that she felt that soon
she would become a part of the glowing chimaera, her limbs
would be added to the arsenal of its bones, her soft lips
would separate and become one more set of entrances into
its heaving, moist carne. The entity possessed a fluctuating,
energetic reality.

G, she mouthed, G, G, G, G, G, G...

Playfully, the beast assumed the shape of the letter G
and then its smooth back began to separate and the letter to
fragment. And then it assumed the form of the word, *aguil-
lanneuf.* A gift, a cry. And all through these transmogrifica-
tions, the music beast remained in some way, parametrical,
paradoxical, unchanged. Blood horses. Norman justice. *Ja-
mais un coup de des,* the beast said to her, and she understood, in light, that to refuse to remain static was to baulk at
God.

And she felt the hygre pull her into its substance, into the blood-lamps of sacrifice. The thing began to move towards her. And then she touched the beast's back and she realised that its skin was made of cotton. Repulsed, she stepped back. Mark inched like a serpent across the cold stone. He had other women - that was understood - curvaceous women who bled with the moon and whose bodies moved like the sea. *It's in the genes, you can't avoid it. You're lucky you've got me; without me, you'd be lost, adrift, alone. Starvation is not salvation.* She did not have other men.

Laura thought she heard the rushing of water, or maybe it was just another of the ambient sounds which had begun to swell beneath the transept and which drew her away, out of this labyrinth of the beast. She walked backwards along the corridor and emerged once again into the main chamber. She was sweating furiously. She felt nauseous. All around, the dancers ellipsed with the Clyde dead at their backs. He took her always from behind, through the darkness that lay beneath her tail-bone. He took her as though she were a reptile.

She bustled frantically, this way and that, in an attempt to escape the noise, the nakedness, the terrifying geometrics, but the clubbers had become so closely packed (still, without touching) that wherever she ran, she found only howling walls of skin. She dared not press herself against the bodies; their surfaces were repugnant; and she dashed down one passageway after another, reasoning that one of them, at least, must be the exit. Yet each of the rooms possessed the same, musty smell. *Centuries of vellum, pored over by unwashed, onanising monks. The threshing-floor, burning malt. Majuscule! Water of life!* But again, the images seemed disconnected, not merely from touch but also from this smell of words which she found herself unable to expurgate from her nostrils. Cana on the Clyde. Kentigern, Columba, Harry Lauder. *I am the word, become flesh.* She had been colonised by the Logos, by the reek of old sperm.

She drank from his spine.

She felt that she would faint, or worse, that she might

go mad, if she didn't get out soon. She had no coat, but she
didn't care. She needed fresh winter air, to clear her head, to
wash it free of accumulating demons. Mirrors, scales: scales,
mirrors. He was all-seeing. She needed to begin, again.

She ran towards the sound of running water. I am not
a reptile, she thought. I am a fish and soon I will drown in
the air. At last, she jolted against the envelope of the khoreia.
She ran her palm along its surface, fascinated by the feel of
it on her skin. It possessed the same soft, enveloping texture
as the walls, the tables, the beast. She moved along its fabric, teasing out its caesurae and as she knew it would, at a
certain point the blackness opened, and she was out.

Laura found herself at the base of a curving stairwell.
She sat on the second-bottom step and gulped large
draughts of the damp air. At length, the tightness around
her throat began to ease and her breathing grew steadier.
The stone tasted dank, neglected, yet Laura had regained a
sense of precision; she was alone, and the silence was black.

She flinched, as her left arm touched an irregularity in
the wall. *Fat bitch*, she thought, *the flesh is spreading.* But
then she ran the index finger of her right hand over the wall
and found that like an heretical, chiromantic sculptor, she
was able to pull shapes from the flat stone, was able to feel
its screams.

The ceiling was so low, she had to climb on hands-
and-knees up the spiral staircase. Every step was bounded
at right angles by a vertical trumeau and by the figures that
came to stand between these portals, one for each step. And
then, as the faces emerged from the stone, Laura began,
once again, to hear music, though now it was a dissonant
harmony of choirs. She was troubled by the sense of having
missed some vital piece of sound, something that would
allow her to construct reasons, but she was jarred out of this
by a hammering of footsteps, emanating from somewhere behind her. She felt the cord of panic tighten around her
throat. Everything was closing in; the floor, the walls, the
roof which she could not see but was able to feel, and everywhere, filling up the air, was stone. Suffocating stone. One

blow followed the next in a lunatic rhythm, a rhythm
that seemed to say: *You're nothing, you're nothing, you're
nothing.*

Agonisingly, she forced herself to shift her bloodied,
stiffened knees of skin-and-bone; yet there must be some fat
there too, mustn't there, lying beneath the integument, fat
which, no matter what she did, she was unable to extrude
from her body, fat that enveloped her, fat that became her.
His breath was on her back, her hair, she could feel him
through the tear in the cloth, the fissure which had been
opened as she had ripped herself away from his dancing
form; in the fracture, the long-dead of the Queen's Park
bandstand, the buckram soldiers of the glass house, the
pungency of dark wood and ticking clocks and always, the
virgin-girls with their big, moist, bowl eyes; perhaps her
shadow was still in the antechamber, dancing with Stan
Laurel.

She tasted warm salt, and realised that she was weeping, that she was blind with weeping as, with every footstep,
the grinding bones of her knees mingled with the hammering
of his boots and with each swing of the hammer, the pounding in her chest grew more frenzied. She sobbed as she
climbed, and her tears flowed in streams down onto the dark
slabs and ran between the cracks. Yet happiness flooded her
being, happiness that came from the punishment of the
flesh. A circlet of leaves, a severed spine, blood in the river.
Penitence.

As she rounded yet another twist of the spiral, Laura
felt his hand on her shoulder, on the skin, in the place where
the cloth had been rent. She recognised the touch of him in
the wound, she knew his smell, the scent of old blood, the
odour of a power for which she longed. The threshing-floor, a
thousand coarse-faced, apron'd workers. Still on her knees,
as she had so many times before, she slung her spine with
gravity, allowed the snake-jaws to part, and then she twisted
her neck round, half-expecting her hair to be gathered-up
like fleece in his powerful hands and coiled into a rope
strong enough to snap the saddle-bone. But he was not

there and silence reigned.

The stench of blood had grown so strong, she felt she might choke on it. She'd never been a vomiter; her demon resided in the need to modulate energy for matter. Energy, power. His absence had always been more terrifying than his presence. Unless we are tested, those which we imagine to be our virtues are merely fanciful conceits; only sin can be acted on out of its own accord, and so, it is only our vices which are sincere. Everything else is just fear. The master was afraid of the slave; the count, of the minstrel; the duelist, of the woman; the woman, of herself. Hazel into oak. This edifice rendered momentary strength to Laura. *I no longer fear you! I'm free!* she called out to the darkness behind her, but her voice sounded tremulous and its echo fell away into nothing.

She turned away from him and continued to crawl upwards, up and up, towards the sky, and as she rounded another bend, she felt a blast of freezing air hit her in the face. A darkness-without-border welled around her, intoxicating in its immensity. The singing of the choir had faded and only the plaintive drone of an old viol issued from somewhere - from which direction, she couldn't tell - a single, repeated note; she tried to grasp it, to hold the sound as, over the years, he had held the power and she inhaled and felt the note diffuse through her body.

Carefully, she rose, steadying herself against the lintel. The music loosened and eased away her stiffness, her pain and the blood at her knees. Above her, the stars burned, blindingly - countless stars, more than she had ever seen - while below, the cityscape moved slowly in light. Laura extended her arms as though she were opening out a pair of giant leather scrolls. The breeze sifted strands of her hair, and the sweat began to dry. She drank in great mouthfuls of the night, and felt herself grow lighter...lighter, so felt that soon she might weigh nothing at all and would be able to fly, to leap off the tower of the malt kiln and to soar high above the metropolis, to leave Mark trapped in stone and to be, at last, empty. Weightless.

She stepped forwards, once, twice, and felt herself wobble. She held onto one of the balustrades which protruded from the fat buttresses. *Between earth and sky, I am.* A shape darker than the night loomed before her. Laura felt only air and space, as though the balustrade along which she walked was a narrow plank, and she was drawn to the emptiness. Yet as she came closer, the shape blotted out more and more of the sky and of the city until it came to fill everything... the air, the past, the music, and then Laura stopped moving forwards, teetered a little, on the edge. She reached out. Metal. Drew back. Touched again. The sound had changed, had become simpler, harder, from a chord to a note: G. It was the note of the viol, the sleek of Roman gold, the sound which comes, deep in the night from the other side of the window. Hogmanay, the holy day.

The stars radiated an intense cold and Laura felt her body begin to freeze outwards from the old wound. Diamond-cut. Pure sound. Innervation. Her voice would be her triumph, her jactance, her future. Her skin would not bleed into the wind; she was the wind, she was the stars. Mark had failed completely to possess her. And now Laura would begin to take back that which had always been hers. She was speaking, but she had no words. She felt the bones and flesh of the church swell inside her body, its stone integument, its arched spine, its opened vulva. Laura was the tidal bore in the Abhainn Chluaidh; up there, on the tower, she was invisible, her power was absolute.

The bell began to move.

To swing, slowly to and fro, scattering stars as it went. Laura felt the wind of its course sweep against her skin. *Perhaps, like a gargoyle I should sing forever across the darkness, and keep him away...*

But he was there, before her, by the swinging, darkening currach, he was making it sail through the air. The mover of metal, of sword, of spear, of bullet. Mark, Marco, Marcus. He was the one who had trapped the snake, who had turned its flesh into his metal. And she had been cast adrift. She felt his shade wrap like a skin around the bell and a spasm of fear reflexed through her body. She screamed at the shade, at the henbane bell, at the night, but her cry was drowned as the bell swung.

She clapped her hands over her ears, but it was no use. At the third boom, she gave up and allowed the sound to flow through her belly and spill from her opened mouth.

Her body quivered with each stroke. At the seventh, flakes of snow began to dance like white butterflies across her eyes.

Beneath her, the burning malt rose from the kiln and beneath the kiln lay an immense iron Crucifix and below that, the countless, seething bodies of plague victims. Clyde-built.

On the tenth peal, Laura heard both their names in music. Beneath the arc of the swaying bell, the air was tensile, unresolved, yet she had lived always in this state, had never quite been able to soar into resolution. She screamed, an atonal, wordless scream which vibrated inside her skull as the metal raged without. The viol had long since ceased to play and her breathing was punctuated by only the cold, pulsing darkness and the single cadence formed by the slow swing of metal through air. Her mouth was open, and her voice was silent, intense, liminal through stone. The bell glowed as though it was molten and she had the urge to leap off the parapet and to cling onto the smooth skin of the iron womb; she would stick like an insect to its surface and would merge completely with its substance. Surely she had proved her love, a thousand times over. It was time to reap her reward. Untrammelled energy. Bean shith.

Her feet began to lose their footing on the worn, slippery stone. She wheeled her arms through the air and watched as the snow fell more rapidly about her shape, and she wondered what her shadow would look like as it fell to earth. Every muscle in her body was taut, pulled to the extreme. As Laura felt the pure note of the twelfth peal die, her mother's face as it had been before the madness flitted before her and she became aware of her own breathing. For Laura, there had never been any asylum. But then she smelled the breeze rising from the depths of the river and the black silk of the night moved over her.

And there, by the edge of the dark, clear water, Laura opened her mouth and stretched backwards so that her spine shadowed the curve of the bell. And when her chest felt as though it was about to explode, she let out a high-pitched scream which echoed through stone and metal and filled the old church with light. She could not hear her voice, but she could feel its pitch vibrate in the bones, which, one day would be dust shadows and which would dance across the forest glade and be caught in the pink gleams of the morning sun. Her eyes still wide open, her throat, turned to that of a bird, Laura filled the night with her G *minor* solo. She longed to cleave the dark waters, to feel what lay beyond...

## Omu Prin & Me

## Daibhidh Martin

Omu Prin felt it belonged to him - the gentle cry of restless birds hovering close by and the regular conversation of the sea, wiping the taupe canvas clean for another day. As he stood in the middle of the beach surrounded by the flotsam and jetsam he would lift his eyes to the stars and sing a song from beginning to end. He would dance erratically as he sang, pausing occasionally, as though inviting a response from the audience of seabirds. I was enchanted, watching a sixty-year-old man dance so carefree.

When I asked to meet him he told me to come to *Traigh Fhada* at 3am. I arrived about half past two according to my pocket watch - an heirloom left to me by my grandfather. It was the first birthday present his wife had ever bought him and he often told me how he had looked on its face as a window to the life that waited for him beyond the war. When his heart started failing at the age of sixty-eight he knew he didn't have long to live and one bright summers day asked to see me. He was lying in bed and started telling me jokes and stories when I sat down next to him. I was only eight years old. He clumsily grabbed my hand and pressed the watch into it. His eyes looked into mine and as he let go of the watch I felt like I understood something but wasn't sure what. He made me promise to take care of the watch and look upon it as a window.

It read quarter to three when I heard the lilting voice of Omu Prin singing an old Gaelic song as he made his way across the beach.

"Far am faca mi an òigh
*Where as a young man I saw the maid*
Thuit mi òg anns a' ghràdh"
*with whom I fell in love*

His voice carried easily on the light breeze that caressed the shore. His steps were measured but his performance had all the elegance of a bear trying to claw a salmon from a river. I shouted to him but he didn't respond until he had finished singing. After his routine he paused for a moment, as though he were allowing his faithful fans the chance to applaud his majestic display. When he raised his head he asked in a soft voice, "What is it that I can do for you?"

"Well," I said, slightly disoriented by his grand entrance, "My grandfather told me I could visit you."

Omu remained silent.

"He bought one of your gates and said that he knew you well," I offered.

"His name was Campbell MacDonald," I said, sure that the mention of the name would provoke a response, but his gaze was fixed beyond my shoulders. All of a sudden he threw his arms open and started dancing again. I stood there in silence as he entertained someone, maybe the seagulls, maybe just himself.

When he finished he bent down and filled his palm with sand and asked me "How many grains?"

"I don't have a clue, maybe ten thousand!"

"That's the thing isn't it," he said. "You reach a point when you think you have all the answers, or at least you're supposed to, then you discover you don't have them, and you panic. When all we need to do is try and count sand." Now it was my turn to remain silent.

"A sandcastle was the first thing I ever built by myself," Omu continued, "and I was devastated when I went back the next day and saw it had been steamrollered by the tide. I wouldn't go back to the beach for months. Then one day I realised that each day I can start over again," he said triumphantly.

I nodded slowly, before realising he wasn't looking at me anymore so I just said "Uh huh," in a way that showed I didn't fully understand.

He started to walk across the beach picking up

bits of wood as he found them and so I copied him, hoping for more.

"Is it really this driftwood you use to make your gates?" I asked him.

He stopped walking and turned to face me. The way he looked at me as he began to speak was otherworldly.

"It was the same year my wife and I were married, we had just built the house I live in and we were looking forward. We were twenty-three. She was swimming in the sea and was pulled out by a rip tide. For years I wouldn't set foot on the beach and then I remembered the sandcastles. Every night since then I have come down to this beach and collected whatever washes ashore and used it to build my gates."

"Oh, I'm sorry, I didn't realise."

"This was the last place we were together," he said. "So what washes ashore is a gift to me from my wife. Some nights I can hear her voice dancing around my ears with the wind. You know, I've always had enough wood wash ashore to make a living from my gates. The wood that survives wreckage is the strongest."

"I'd never thought of it like that." I responded, happy just to be able to say something.

He started to walk back across the beach and, pointing at a large log still being caressed by the foam, said "Help me take that wood back to my house, if you have the time?"

"No problem," I said, letting out a little smile.

The early sun was threatening to spoil the fog that clung to the coastline as we approached Omu's house. It was quite hard to make out the details in the faint light but from a distance it looked as though parts of the house were moving with the wind. When we drew near I could see that all manner of bizarre objects had been screwed onto the outside of his house. Among them was a frayed section of a fishing net draped from the base of the chimney, a green wellie attached to the gable end and an old steering wheel protruding from the window sill, which had been attached in such a way that it still turned.

"Just drop it there," he said, pointing to a giant pile of

wood. I found it hard to believe that all this wood had washed up on the beach but couldn't formulate the question fast enough, without accusing him of lying, and then the moment was gone.

"In case you're wondering about the outside of my house, that was my wife's pastime. She used to bring all sorts of crap back from the beach when I wasn't around. She said it made the house more personal," Omu said, before letting out a little laugh. "She put all this up in less than a year; imagine what the house would look like if she was still alive."

I didn't really feel I could laugh, but I concocted a noise somewhere between a laugh and a sniff instead.

"She was the most beautiful person I ever knew," he said, beaming.

"We'd better have a cup of tea to warm us up."

"That'd be great," I said, overenthusiastically. "I start to get palpitations if I don't have tea at least every second hour. A true islander."

As Omu brewed a pot on the stove I sat in one of the old wooden chairs, arranged symmetrically around an open space where a kitchen table should be.

"If the sun breaks through it'll be a lovely morning," I said sleepily, before taking another mouthful of tea. I wasn't surprised to have one of my questions treated with silence so I just continued to slump in my chair and drift away. It could only have been a matter of minutes later when I heard Omu hammering away at the wood we had just taken home. Not wanting to appear lazy, I left my unfinished cup of tea and went outside to join him.

"I was only twelve years old when I made my first gate," he began without looking up from the wood. "My mother had a patch where she grew vegetables, mostly potatoes, and every year the neighbours dog would destroy some of it, so finally she asked my father to make a gate to keep the dog out. Well, time kept rolling on and my father always had something better to do so I decided to make it myself. I collected all the wood I could find and was about to start nailing it together when my father came out. He said I was being disrespectful and gave me the wrong side of his hand before taking the wood for the fire."

He paused for a moment, as if playing it over in his head.

"I'd never been so determined to do anything in my life before I made that gate. It was as much to spite my father as to please my mother. It's funny," he laughed to himself. "It was only two days after that my father was made redundant and left us behind. I mean, physically he was still there but all he did was drink and curse the stupid skipper who 'couldn't find a monkfish if you stuck it to his arse.' I remember the look on my mother's face when she saw the first gate I made and when she cooked the first of the new potatoes. Said it was the most beautiful gate she'd ever seen."

"The gate you made for my grandfather looks as though it could have been made yesterday," I said, as casually as I could.

"I made it from driftwood just like this," he said, raising the log in his hands.

As the morning light grew I noticed a gate peering out from a wooden boat that sat behind Omu's shed.

"Is that where you store your gates when they're ready?" I asked him, pointing to the boat.

"No, that's one I made for my wife," he said smiling.

"Every year on her birthday I make a gate with my name carved into the bottom and then row out to sea and drop it in the ocean. When I let the gate go I pray it will drift into good hands." A smile broke across his weathered face as he gazed out on the Atlantic Ocean, "there's nothing between here and America," he said, before returning his attention to the splintered piece of wood in his hands.

I sat there in a daydream for a few moments, imagining gardens on the east coast of America with gates signed by Omu Prin.

## Playground Rules

### Doug Johnstone

It's twenty years since I've been in a school playground, and I'm going to puke or pass out or have a fucking stroke or something. I feel the Wee Man's brittle fingers in my grip as we pass through the gate into the orchestrated mania that only large packs of kids can produce.

'Too tight, Daddy.'

I look down. The Wee Man's mouth is a grimacing line. 'What?'

He looks at me like I'm an idiot.

'You're hurting my hand.'

I ease off. I'm suddenly very conscious of my heart and lungs pumping and my legs moving, and I worry about how I'm going to keep propelling myself forward.

Two older boys are pushing a runt down a hill and filming it on their phones. A bam with a mohawk and earrings spits at some pristine girls and laughs. Swarms of smaller kids buzz around like angry bluebottles.

I look at the Wee Man. Is he as freaked out as me? His face is placid, blank, those green eyes of his, so like his mum's, either world-weary or innocent or scared or sly or fuck knows what – I have no clue anymore.

I have no clue about anything. I can't remember getting up this morning. How the hell did we have breakfast, get dressed and get out the door on time? I'm not even sure why I'm being allowed to do this. Shouldn't someone responsible step in and take control of this shitstorm?

My days are an insomniac blur, my mind thick as porridge. In comparison, the nights are crystalline in their brutal honesty. The Wee Man is suffering from 'night terrors', according to the doctor. That made me snigger, despite the situation we find ourselves in, because a scene from *The*

*Simpsons* flashed across my mind, – Homer writhing on the floor screaming 'Cobras! Argh!' That's me, Dad of the Year, laughing at a cartoon instead of caring about my own precious progeny. Add it to the long list of things to feel fucking great about.

Another flash from *The Simpsons* as we walk through the playground past shrieking harpies and hollering chimps – Bart starting an online cartoon about Homer called 'Angry Dad'. Yes, quite. My not-so-subtle subconscious. In that episode, Bart falls victim to the dot.com boom and bust, shouting incredulously at the end: 'Bubbles can burst?'

Sarah and I laughed watching that, sitting on the sofa, me drunk on Chilean red, her exhausted but content, I think, both of us stroking the bump that would become the Wee Man three months later. We were in our own un-burstable bubble back then.

The Wee Man wakes eight or nine times a night, screaming and crying, his world collapsing around him, snot and tears streaking his face. He's inconsolable, but I try to console him anyway, what the fuck else can I do? But that only makes things worse. Eventually I lose my temper and shout at him. Angry Dad, indeed.

As a result of all this, the Wee Man has moved into the marital bed. What would the teachers and parents around here think of that? A grown man and a four-year-old boy sleeping together. Fuck them, they don't know.

It doesn't take a genius to work out the root of the night terrors. If I could force them on myself instead of him, I would. I certainly feel up for a bout of primal screaming in the darkness of the night. But I don't. I just lie there, numb with whisky and self-pity, waiting for the Wee Man's next emergence from his murky subconscious.

It's two months and twelve days since the incident. Listen to me, 'the incident'. That's the fucking grief counsellor talking. Everyone knows about grief, right, the different stages? Is it five or seven? I got handed the leaflet at some point, but the details are sketchy. Could seven stages be like the Magnificent Seven? Or the Seven Dwarfs? Yeah, Dopey is

Denial, Sleepy could be Depression. Grumpy would be Anger and Happy would have to be Acceptance. But where did that leave the others? What the hell do you do with Sneezy? And where are the Wee Man and myself in all this? He seems to swither between Confusion and Denial fifty times a day. I've skipped Denial and Bargaining and gone straight for a cocktail of Anger and Depression. Although the truth is, that's not much different from how I was before 'the incident', so fuck knows. Maybe it would be easier if I'd been a better husband and father before *you know what*. I don't think we can even call it 'the accident', not with the court case pending.

We stayed for the weekend at an overpriced hotel on the banks of Loch Tay. The Wee Man was with the in-laws, the idea was a last bit of pampering for Sarah before the arrival of baby number two. It was her shout, and since she earned vastly more than my meagre freelance photography scramblings, who was I to argue? All I had to do was get us there and back, feed her chocolates and rub her feet. Confectionary and foot massage I could manage, but evidently not the driving. We hit a Forestry Commission van head on at a blind corner on the single-track road that hugs the south edge of the loch. I'd had a glass of wine at lunch, enough to register on the breathalyser but not enough to put me over the limit. Sarah and the unborn child were killed on impact, according to the coroner. I spent two days in hospital with cuts, bruises and mild concussion.

My relative wellbeing was an affront to everyone, myself most of all. How dare I still be alive? I was charged with careless driving, after some forensic nerds established how fast I was going from the skid marks. That and the blood alcohol didn't add up to a pretty picture, but the fact I was still under the limit meant I was 'careless' rather than 'dangerous' or 'reckless'. I can't even go to jail. I can only get a fine and points on the licence, which is just another in the endless line of insults to Sarah.

'Daddy! Too *tight*.'

I look at the Wee Man again. His eyebrows are raised

like a cartoon character's, in that way small kids over-compensate when mimicking the facial expressions of adults. He actually rolls his eyes, which makes me smile. His hair's too long, but I've been unable to contemplate getting it cut. Sarah always used to deal with that. Maybe he'll never get a haircut again, in memory of dear old Mummy.

Apart from his basic school uniform, the Wee Man has Super Mario Bros. badges on his jacket, is wearing a *Ben 10* backpack and carrying his *Spiderman* lunchbox. He hasn't ever played *Super Mario Bros.*, how the hell does he know so much about it?

Sarah and I initially resisted all that branded crap when he was a baby, holding on to some half-baked principle which was never explicitly stated, and which seems archaic now. Because very quickly, once they're socialising at any basic level, there's no avoiding it. It came as a shock to both of us, the Wee Man impregnated with ideas by older kids and staff, thoughts we had no control over, our little baby dragged away from us on a tide of social influence we couldn't stem.

We reach the infants' playground now, where they line up to go into class. Welcome to a lifetime of peer pressure, Wee Man, an eternity of trying and failing to fit in. It feels like I'm leading a trusting, blank-eyed cow through a slaughterhouse door. I'm killing him. We're all killing our children with this bullshit, why the fuck do we do it?

I look around at the other families. Who the hell are these people? I used to laugh at these morons, mock their affordable suburban homes in an unfashionable corner of Edinburgh. But I can't take the piss out these poor bastards anymore. I have the same hangdog expression, the same gut stretching my T-shirt, the same boot cut Gap jeans, the same cheap trainers, the same air of nervous exhaustion, the same the same the same.

In fact I'm worse than them, because I still think I'm better somehow, which only leads to pathetic, vicious self-loathing, something I'm all too familiar with these days, thank you very much.

And it's only going to get worse. Time is the great piss-taker, stretching off into infinity. And all the sitting at home, wanking your flaccid cock over porn featuring women who look like your dead wife, right down to the pregnant bump, is not going to fill that void.

I'm not even really grieving for her and the baby, not completely. Part of me is grieving for myself, the life I've lost, the control that escapes me now. And then there's the Wee Man to consider. I've robbed him of his family and childhood.

Talk your fucking way out of that one, grief counsellor.

We approach the line outside the classroom door, and I feel tremors through my body. I look at the Wee Man's face, now showing signs of trepidation.

'I don't want to go in, Daddy.'

I don't fucking blame you, Wee Man, I really don't.

I kneel down and smell sour milk on his breath. It's a beautiful smell. I try to keep my voice level.

'It's OK, Wee Man, it'll be fun. And Daddy will be back soon to pick you up and hear all about it, OK?'

'Nooo.' He's jiggling on the spot, like when he needs a piss.

'You'll be fine. Give me a cuddle.'

I hold him too long and too tight. I know I'm doing it but I can't help it. I kiss the top of his head, that long mess of hair soft against my cracked lips. I look away so he doesn't see I'm almost crying, and when I turn back he's staring at me.

I look along the line. All this potential, all these little souls about to have the spirit squeezed out of them. The Wee Man is the smallest kid here. No surprise, since he's also the youngest. But he's a bright spark, and Sarah and I decided not to defer entry, figuring he would go nuts another year at nursery. As it turns out, I couldn't have paid the fees for another year anyway. We had life insurance, bought in an uncharacteristic moment of common sense, but they won't pay out for Sarah, under the circumstances. Along with my inability to drum up work since the crash, well, let's just say we probably won't be in our pebble-dashed suburban utopia much longer.

As I watch the line of kids, a boy with his hair gelled up in a spike shoves in front of the Wee Man. The Wee Man looks at me, upset. I don't know what sort of signal to give him. This is life, I'm afraid, hair-gelled cunts cutting in front of you from now until the fucking grave.

The Wee Man shoves Hair Gel half-heartedly, saying something to him. Hair Gel grabs the front of the Wee Man's coat and shakes him pretty hard, an angry look on his face. The Wee Man rips Hair Gel's hands from his jacket then pushes him in the chest.

It's escalating. I look around for Hair Gel's mum or dad, anyone else paying attention to what the boys are doing. The playground is a sea of nervous faces and mundane chatter.

I turn back and they're wrestling now, clutching and shoving each other. I walk over and separate them.

'That's enough, guys, no pushing.' My voice sounds alien, too high, too strained, not like me at all.

'He pushed in,' says the Wee Man, on the verge of tears.

'No, I didn't,' says Hair Gel.

'You did, I saw you.' This is me talking, although I sound like one of them, a small child waiting to have the world explained to me in all its glorious shitness. 'It's not nice to push in, maybe you should go to the back of the line.' Am I really saying this?

'No,' says Hair Gel with a stubborn face.

'Yes.'

'You're not my dad, you can't make me.'

'Oh, can't I?'

I pull Hair Gel's arm. The look of shock on his face cheers me up no end. He stumbles out of the line towards me as the voices around us grow louder.

'What do you think you're doing?'

I turn and see Hair Gel's mum, same narrow eyes, same thuggish brow, same attitude of entitlement. Her haircut is aggressive, all angles and edges, and she smells of thick, flowery perfume.

'Get your hands off my son,' she says, snatching his arm and dragging him away.

'He pushed in the line.'

'My Jamie wouldn't do that.'

'He did,' says the Wee Man, finding his voice. The sound sends a shiver of joy through me.

Hair Gel's mum turns to him. 'You shut up, I saw you hitting him.'

'Woah,' I say, 'don't talk to my fucking son like that.'

Hair Gel's mum moves closer to me and actually bares her teeth. 'What did you say?'

'You fucking heard me.'

She's so close I can smell her breath now, a bitter mintiness.

'Maybe if you stopped swearing and concentrated on raising your son better, he wouldn't be such a bully.'

My fist drives hard into her face before I know I'm doing it. It connects perfectly with that sharp nose and I feel a crumple under my knuckle as a jolt of pain travels down my arm and electrifies my body. It's as if I'm conducting the primal force of a lightning strike, I'm the centre of immense power. The relief is astonishing, and sickening, and thrilling. Hair Gel's mum has tears in her eyes as she holds her nose, blood spattering onto the concrete at her feet as she reaches in her pocket for a tissue.

The sight of that red spurt reminds me of Sarah, and suddenly the manic noise around us is gone, a deep, reverential hush shrouding everything.

I look around. Everyone is staring at me.

I turn to the Wee Man. His eyes are wet. I look into those eyes – Sarah's eyes – and I still have no idea how much I've lost.

## Overnight Observation

## Helen Lynch

---

She was awful groggy when she came round. The nurse lifted her off the trolley into my arms, taking care to avoid knocking the boxing-glove bandages that covered her hands. Her blue dressing gown was fastened by the top button like a superhero cloak but otherwise she was naked, except for her nappy. I wanted to warm her, though she didn't feel cold. For a moment I held her in front of me and we all looked at her - Cam, the nurse, me - then I climbed into her bed. I left Cam to do the explaining and snuggled her in the crook of my arm.

And there we stayed. When night came we were wheeled regally through the corridor into the night ward. The consultant was a bit concerned, he said, about the amount of mucus on her chest. They'd rather keep her in for observation, just tonight.

'I'll have to stay with her,' I said quickly. 'She's still breast-fed.'

Of course I was very welcome to stay. There was a day-room just along the corridor where the mothers usually found the chairs relatively comfortable.

'I'd rather be in bed with her, if you don't mind. She always sleeps with us at home.' I risked the confession - she was one-and-a-half, after all - but he didn't seem inclined to mess with me.

Cam left me with a sandwich he'd bought. Rachel was still sleeping, though she'd woken briefly and suckled. I lay and thought of her and of my relief. The operation itself was minor. I eased myself away from her enough to sit up and start the sandwich.

There were other kids and their parents in the ward. The boy in the bed next to me had just been told he'd have to stay another night. He was scowling into the hand-held computer game his Dad had given him, glaring his tears into its small screen and fiddling with the knobs. Eventually his Dad - who'd been trying to say that there was nothing for it, but to try and put up with it another night, that he'd see them in the morning and he'd go home tomorrow for sure - told him to stop bleeping that bloody game.

As soon as his parents had gone, he flung the game on the bedside table.

'There's no need for that, Matthew,' said one of the nurses coming on duty.

'He still here?' She asked the other two nurses, jerking her head at Matthew so that they turned round.

Most of the children on this ward had had tonsillectomies. At the far end a girl with long, pale hair was being sick into a bowl.  On the other side of the ward a mother with immaculate lipstick and an expensive-looking checked suit was trying to quiet a whimpering three-year-old who wouldn't lie down. A nurse told the woman to go to the other room, that she'd settle the child. The mother did as she was told, though her look as she moved away from the bed conveyed a mixture of relief and doubt. In the cot directly opposite, a wee boy, even younger than Rachel, was getting his parents to take turns on his toy phone.

The large screen at the end of the ward was showing The Lion King. Rachel woke up, sat up, looked at her bandaged hands, lifted one, then dropped it as though she had forgotten it already.

'Cheese,' she said, looking at my sandwich. 'Mummy eat cheese and bread.' I was thankful she was such a good talker, that at least she could tell me what was going on with her. I fed her most of the sandwich and gave her a drink of water. She seemed quite enlivened and turned at once to the screen: stampeding animals, the wicked lion clawing at his rival at the top of a cliff, the fall, the thundering hooves, the dust, the trampling, the lion cub nuzzling the immobile body of his father. I felt suddenly distressed. Why did they put this stuff on? How on earth was it supposed to help anyone in a post-operative state?

Rachel was riveted, her pupils huge. I tried to distract her with books, with her toy mouse, to pretend that nothing very important was taking place on the screen, but she wasn't fooled.

'What that lion do?'

The wee boy in the cot opposite was vying for her attention. His parents were half letting him and half shushing him, as though they would dearly love some company and entertainment for their son but couldn't be seen to seek it. The child seemed very lively and in a gregarious mood, yet in this open room full of people whom he was clearly dying to get to know, his parents seemed all the more careful to keep to themselves, not to impose.

So I took Rachel over and at once he wanted her to play telephones and involved her in a book-swapping game, while I chatted to his mother. Calum had a testicle that had started to work its way in the wrong direction. His operation was the next day but he was in overnight to help him to fast.

Eventually Calum and Rachel grew so spirited that they wanted to run up and down the ward, so we took them out to let them charge about the corridor - the other mother and I shyly probing one another, remark by remark, each trying not to look more or less permissive than the other.

---

I woke up certain it was day. A trolley was making its way along the ward. I got up and poked my head out through the curtains. The face of the clock above the door at the far end said two o'clock. Not possible. The orderly with the trolley offered me a cup of tea. I took one - I might as well be up for the rest of the night. I felt quite wide awake already. The night-nurses were clustered round the desk in a pool of light. Two had their backs to me. The orderly gave them tea. I'd already drunk some of mine and felt jittery straight away. The orderly was friendly but not chatty- though I felt sped up and ready to talk - and soon moved on to other wards. I sat on the edge of the bed and sipped some more tea.

I lay and listened to the noises of the night beyond my curtains. I thought of the humps in the dark beds and closed my eyes, but at this point Rachel stirred and started rooting for my breast. I turned myself towards her and eased the nipple into her mouth. She was not suffering at all, I thought, glorying in it. This was a normal night for her, smell of Mummy and warm milk coursing down her throat in small, satisfied gulps.

Someone cried out, a faint, strangulated, dreaming cry. Then another voice was calling, desperately, but as if it hardly dared be heard.

'Nurse, nurse.'

The pale-haired girl at the far end, I surmised. There was the unmistakable sound of someone being sick - a sound I knew retrospectively that I'd heard several times in my sleep. Perhaps no one had heard her - should I call from my bed to alert someone... or could I ease the baby... but the clipped tread of one of the nurses proceeded down the ward. There were sounds of gulping and more retching, the puke plootering the sides of the bowl and, to judge by the tutting of the nurse, the front of the child's nightie as well.

'Look at the state of you. D'you think we've endless supplies of fresh nighties? You'll hae tae make dae with that one - here, dab it with this.'

She was about eleven, I remembered, with a clammy face – her long hair dripping down the side of her face like melting wax. I saw her in my mind's eye, a few droukit wisps at her temples, eyes still watering from the effort, blinking, swallowing the bitter remnants down her swollen throat.

The boy in the next bed was moving fretfully, scissoring his legs, thumping his head down on different parts of the pillow, mumbling. One of his covers fell off and I pulled my curtain back on his side and peeped at him.

'Och, leave him,' one of the nurses at the desk told the other, who looked as if she might do something. 'He's aye the same. Stop that, Matthew,' she commanded, and they went on with their conversation.

I'd seen the one with the iron-filings hair register that I was watching. Was this normal for them? I slid my finger into Rachel's mouth to try to break the suction on my breast. She was fast asleep and barely sucking, but she detected the attempt at once and lunged at the retreating nipple and began sucking for all she was worth. Matthew was not an appealing boy. His dark skinhead cut emphasised the rectangular shape of his face, and gave his pallid skin an almost purple tinge. He didn't actually have a bolt through his neck, but he wasn't cute and biddable and he did not want to be there.

The third nurse was back again to join the other two, but almost immediately had to return to the other end of the ward - just as she reached for her cup. The girl was being sick again.

'You'll never be out of here with this carry-on,' the nurse informed her. 'Doctor says you cannae go home unless you keep something down.'

The girl sobbed at this and said something inaudible to me, bringing the explosion.

'You dinnae need your Mum, a great girl like you. Your Mum's at home asleep in her bed, which is where you should be too - you never will be if you won't try to keep your tea inside you. You'll be needing another operation if you go on this wey.'

Above the sound of the pale girl's sniffling, suppressed so that it turned into a cough so painful it came out as a yelp and Mathew grinding his teeth, came the full-throated wail of a much younger child. I thought: this is what Hell sounds like.

The three-year-old had woken. One of the nurses went to her and, to my surprise, spoke to her quite kindly.

'Did you hae a dream? Come on noo, lie doon. You cannae sit up that wey?'

The child clearly would not cooperate, but the nurse remained patient:

'Here then, hae some juice. The doctor says you're tae hae plenty of juice.'

There was a brief silence, during which the child seem-
ingly took a couple of sips of juice from a tippee-cup, then
went back to crying in a heartfelt but directionless way, as if
she didn't quite know where she was. Quite suddenly, as if
by a revelation, she summoned all her woe in a single yowl:
      'Mummy!'
      'You cannae hae Mummy. Here, hae some of your nice
juice,' the nurse responded, trying to poke the spout of the
tippee-cup between the child's teeth. The child continued
wanting Mummy.
      'Why can she not have her Mummy, for God's sake?' I
thought. 'She's only down the corridor.'
      'Open your teeth. Hae some nice juice. You're tae drink
it.'
      The child opened her mouth to wail 'Mu...,' the nurse
tipped the juice, the child spluttered, choked, knocked the
cup with her hand.
      'There, you've got it all... that's a bad girl... you've
wasted your juice. Well, I'll get some mair - you're tae drink it
all. Doctor said. Mummy said.'
      'Mummmeee ...'
      'Mummy's nae here, she's gone tae work, she's sleep-
ing. You dinnae want tae be a bad girl and waken Mummy.'
      The child had settled into a hoarse and rhythmic
screaming. Another nurse arrived as reinforcements and
there were a few moments of struggle:
      'Here, you get her arm... no, hold her,' the child by
now hysterical and terrified.
      'Noo that's enough! What a bad girl to waken all the
girls and boys.'
      Tears streamed down my face. 'She wants her
Mummy, for Christ's sake. Why shouldn't she? For the love
of God, go and get her fucking Mummy.' My head was
screaming so loudly that it took me a moment to realise that
I had not bellowed the words in actuality. I was frightened
lest Rachel should wake up into this horror, yet I felt the pull
pull pull on my breast that seemed to go on forever. Should I
offer to go and fetch the mother? Should I just do it? I didn't

actually know where the mothers were exactly. What if I left the room and Rachel woke up, as in this noise and disturbed atmosphere she was almost bound to do, woke to find me not there, cried out, drew the attention of the nurses...? Were I to intervene they would know at once what it meant, what the stakes were.

To my amazement I succeeded in disengaging myself from Rachel. By this time, several other children in the ward were clearly awake. I had to sound reasonable. I presented myself at the child's bedside:

'Would you like me to run along and get her Mum?' I suggested helpfully.

The nurse who had the child locked in what seemed like a full Nelson looked over her shoulder:

'We'll settle her. There's nae need.'

'I'm sure if I was her Mum I'd want fetched,' I persisted, thinking of the check-suited lady. The second nurse looked at me. She knew a power struggle when she saw one, but she also saw that I was no real opponent for her. Without knowing anything, she knew I was not ready, and her voice was gritty:

'You bide there. We'll sort her oot, never you mind.'

The wee girl was quieter now, partly from exhaustion. The smallest whimper from behind Rachel's curtains and I slunk back to my bed, while the child's crying went on, though softer now, for another age as I suckled my baby, shielding my own flesh and blood in my arms.

There was a brief lull. The nurses gathered again at their table, drank their cold tea and got quite chatty. I eavesdropped shamelessly, straining my ears, hating them, convicting them on every word. Pensions was their main subject, schemes for getting the best possible one, comparing arrangements they'd made, their husbands' pension options and so on. One, it emerged, was married to a policeman, another to a prison officer.

A wail from the cot opposite: Baby Calum. This time I was prepared. I would tell his mother, come what may. I *knew* her. Yet they fell on him, crowing, exclaiming, scooped

him out of the cot and bore him off to their lair by the desk.
Fortunately, he seemed quite happy with all the attention
and only rarely showed signs of returning to grief.

'You're bonny, y'are so.'

'I see you. I see you, smiler.'

He was passed from lap to lap - 'Come tae your Auntie
Jean' - as they went into raptures over his blue, blue eyes.
What a handsome boy he was with that blond hair and those
eyes. What a fine-looking mannie he'd make.

I lay in the bed, fists clenched, but he seemed to have
dozed off on one of their shoulders, if their cooings of satis-
faction were anything to go by. I relaxed a bit, just as one of
them said:

'I think his nappy's wet, Jean.' There were sounds of
nappy-patting. I was scunnered. Who would wake a baby
they've just pacified, wake a sleeping baby, for *that*? Sure
enough, Calum objected robustly to the nappy change. Still,
at last he was quiet and back in his cot.

Matthew was still tossing about, muttering and fever-
ish. Another blanket fell to the floor. I got up and went to his
bedside, replaced the blanket and put my hand on his hot
forehead.

'Dinnae bother wi' him,' a nurse advised me from the
desk. 'He's full o' trouble.'

'I'm sure he doesn't do it just to be annoying,' I said
levelly in my best 'I know just what you're about' voice, turning my head to look them, I hoped meaningfully.

Matthew was sleeping more calmly, but I'd not been
back in my bed five minutes when the slightest sign of re-
newed restlessness had two of them at his side. They'd better
things to do than wait on him all night, they said.

'Why did you nae tell us you was wanting the toilet?'
one of them demanded.

Matthew was barely awake, but they yanked him into
a sitting position.

'I *doant*.'

'You do so,' said the other, and together they had him
under the elbows, swung him out of bed and frog-marched

him to the toilet, he protesting as the door banged shut. They didn't come out for a long time. He was still crying when he got back into bed.

On the other side of me, a girl of about five started to moan. I pulled the corner of my curtain back:

'Shh, sweetheart, shh,' I whispered. 'Go back to sleep.' She turned to face me, gave me one wide-eyed look and dozed off.

'Oh thank God,' I thought, and must have slept. Another trolley. More steps, the light a rinsed-out version of the night-time grey which in hospital passes for morning. The day-nurses were at the desk, two ridiculously rosy-cheeked, fresh-faced young women, one sporting a plump, squishy chignon, the other a glossy bob, looking like teenagers from an Australian soap. A benign-looking older woman was moving among the beds, perching on the ends, asking the children about their cuddly toys, 'cheering them up'.

Rachel seemed perky and content with her surroundings, toddling after the older nurse to display her toy mouse, then over to call on an equally cheery Calum, whose parents looked ill-slept and apprehensive. I resolved to clype to the snub-nosed doctor with the upper-class accent whom I'd already seen bounding with youthful efficiency around the ward. She wore her white coat unbuttoned so that it flew out to both sides and her stethoscope bounced on her chest.

I started to explain. Was I making a complaint? Was I seeking some particular outcome? I focused on Matthew. She looked at me tolerantly, but with faint bemusement, stopped to remove a bit of fluff from her cashmere sweater, and assured me that it was her understanding that Matthew *would* be going home, subject to examination and provided he'd eaten breakfast.

'Well, if it's in the balance at all, please bear in mind what I've said. Your night staff really aren't very nice to him and I'm sure he'll get better a lot faster at home.' With this lame ending, I shuffled off.

Rachel had found an older girl willing to build towers for her so she could knock them down with a swipe of her giant paw. Matthew was the only one still sat at the table in the day-room, two triangles of toast on the plate before him. Rachel dived into the Wendy House. I squatted beside the boy.

'I know it's awful sore but you've got to do this to get home. Let's count while you swallow, then it won't seem so long.' He nodded and took his first bite. It took ages but we counted each mouthful down.

Cam arrived, the doctor gave the all-clear and we went to the foyer for our taxi. Sitting on my knee in the car, batting her father's upheld hands with her boxing glove bandages and crowing, our baby, intact. No trauma for her, apparently. Yet my insides ground and juddered with every gear-change, every jolt of the car, and there seemed no surface cool enough for me to lean my forehead on.

## Beefcake

## Kirstin Innes

---

You should always arrange to meet in a neutral, busy public place. That was the first thing they told you, and they'd say it again and again throughout the application process till it stuck in your head like an advertising jingle, trailing genteel implications of warning and caution with it. It kept her alert but not off-puttingly jumpy. They knew what they were doing.

A neutral-busy-public-place. She always suggested train stations, would arrive fifteen minutes early (because nobody likes to feel they're being stood up) and stand in the same place by the door of the same newsagent chain. She would finger the red flower in her lapel, raise her eyes up to the same posters on the same hoardings and feel the same discreet, anxious movements of travellers bump gently up against her, whether she was in Edinburgh or Dundee or Aberdeen or Perth.

Glen was there to greet her today, as he sometimes was, thick-lashed, bovine-placid. They did like to chuck him at the tourists. Across the concourse, above her head, a young female rump (one pert, globular buttock wriggling playfully out of the bottom of tiny pale-lemon shorts) pushed a chain of luxury gyms. Men's eyes flicked up and over the arse, an automatic reaction, and their women, trailing along behind with the kids and the luggage and already guilt-greased by January, would catch them, would flinch. Glen alone looked straight ahead.

They'd been introduced a couple of years ago, by the same expensive-sounding English woman who breathed oozy luxury over the Markies ads:

- Glen is from Scotland, the woman had told her, cleaving him up in appreciation.

He's lean, fit, and *tasty*.

Glen had smiled, then turned and stomped off across an actual glen into a sunset, the camera clinging to his pecs through his t-shirt before zooming friskily up his kilt for a cheeky wee glimpse of taut thigh meat.

Glen was that antiseptic kind of tall/dark/handsome you got in catalogues. Not a streak of the badness in him.

*At's a nice boay,* her mum would have said, on the sofa with a bottle, while she curled up in embarrassment. *Aye Debbie, you could do worse than a man like that, hen.*

Not her type. Not at all. Still, something had made her lean close to the screen, inhaling the booze back off her own home-thickening accent.

- Glen. Glen. It's no exactly a very Scottish name, is it?

Glen took it, though. Just kept on tucking appreciatively into a perfectly rare steak. On the splitscreen his plukey grey-skinned co-star spilled chips down his top.

- Barry here doesn't, ah, take such good care of himself, the posh lady said, easing good-humoured despair into her voiceover as housewives on sofas across the country tittered audibly.

Tee hee. Aren't men dreadful. All except for Glen and his fine Highland meat. And the logo came up.

---

At her back, a small dry cough.

- Ah. Excuse me. Olivia?

Educated Edinburgh. One of the good, fee-paying merchant schools, and then possibly Glasgow University, now working in law or finance, at least forty-five. She adjusted the shape of her mouth to the necessary accent and turned round.

He was smaller than her in her heels and weedier than you'd think from that well-fed Rotary Club of a voice, fine gingery down over a freckled scalp, the dark crimson rosebud tucked into a classy grey suit. Familiar, from somewhere.

- Charles. Hello.

She eased out the A and flattened the R. *Chaals.* You got them with the accent. Let them speak first, then trickle it down or buff it up till you were equals. No-one was intimidated, no-one felt superior. Before, before this, she'd laughed in pubs with people, said over and over, oh, my accent's a right tart. Ha, ha.

Ha, ha.

His eyes did the familiar sweep, the tits-legs-face, then stuck, bulging, at something above her head. That fucking bum.

- Anyway. Yes. Right. Let's just. Just.

He aimed a thumb at the air behind him.

- Are we taking a cab?

- We are. Yes.

Glen saw them silently off from his brightly-lit silver frame, his sleeve rolled up to reveal hefty forearm, curled casually on a fence. Beside him, the after-shot, a burly prime steak, sex-pink at the centre in ruddy tones that matched his skin, sliced and curled casually on a plate. Christ, they weren't even pretending any more. She savoured the richness of the idea, still bloody, on her tongue. God, she was hungry.

*Chaals* ushered her quickly across the concourse and into a taxi, one small hand nudging the curve of her back to hurry her.

He climbed up into the cab first, neither held the door nor offered to help her with her tiny overnight case, just snapped a placename out at the driver. Her mother's voice roared *and whit do you say?* but she resisted the urge to tack a conciliatory *please* on for him. Sitting down, they were the same height.

- Is that the hotel?

He didn't look at her.

- Yes. The restaurant is excellent, I hear. Contemporary Scottish cuisine but a French chef, of course. Michelin starred. All locally sourced produce; organically-reared beef and just *the* freshest seafood.

Each word clipped from his jaw.

- Well, that sounds wonderful. I must confess, I don't know this part of the country very well. You're - more experienced?

The sex came from her gullet. He flushed, and stared out of the window, showing her a bony, all-too recognisable profile, and something clicked in her head. Ah.

- Around here, I mean?
- I've only visited on business.
- Are you here on business this weekend?
- Could you take a right here, driver.
- Beautiful area. It must be nice to get the chance to come back. For pleasure.
- Indeed.

Silence. Head modestly down, kept her smile neutral and her face small, just let him project whatever he wanted on. His voice snapped out and she jumped.

- So. Ah. I understand you have, ah. Worked as a model?

They always asked that, because she'd put it on her profile. It got good responses. Men liked models. And it wasn't really a lie. Not too much of a lie.

-  Commercial work, mostly.

Mistake. That nippy wee cough again and this time there was all the judgement of the Church of Scotland Assembly in it, as if he couldn't contain himself, his mind nudging and winking and teasing every dirty possible innuendo out of the word.

- Book covers, she said. Stock photography sites. Jewellery, sometimes.

The words just sat there in the cab between them, not quite covering her. Her stomach rumbled, and she smiled to apologise.

- So, what do you do, Charles? For a living?
- Why would you want to know that?
- Because I'm interested.

He just looked at her.

- But you're quite right, of course. Absolutely none of my business.

He indicated the menu.

- Shall we just-?

She kept smiling. That was the other thing they repeated. Keep smiling. Keep smiling.

It was a good looking menu, to be fair, and she was ravenous.

- We'll have the '87 Burgundy, he said, same businessy tone he'd dealt the driver.

- No starters. I'm going to have the confit of duck. And for the la—

—the, eh.

—my, ah.

The waiter was trying his hardest to hold back a smirk. Aw hon, she thought, now you've just given us both away. He coughed, reddened, straightened up.

- Perhaps the monkfish?

Usually, she let them order for her. Made them feel good about it. But this one. She looked up over the menu at him, thought of him goggling away at that arse in the station. Monkfish. Flabby white fishflesh claggit in a cream sauce. Every restaurant had to have an option for unadventurous diners. It was also the cheapest dish on the menu.

- Filet mignon, she said. Rare. Bloody, and she smiled all the judgement off the waiter's mouth.

Charles' arid wee face wrinkled.

- I just found myself *craving* some red meat, she said at him, honey sliding down her throat. Do you ever, ah, get that feeling?

He shifted his skinny backside about in the chair.

- You don't - mind, Charles?

That *cough*.

- I'll be right back, she said.

Slink. Slink. Across the floor in three. He might not have been watching her walk, but everyone else was, and he knew it.

For all the restaurant's cut glass and crystal, its dark-leaved palm fronds and leather, the toilets were terrible.

Cracked tiles and that cheap frazzling light. There was

a sharp draft from under the single formica stall, the sort of weak thing you could kick down wi one sturdy boot.

*Fur coat, nae knickers,* her mother muttered. Yeah. Shut up, maw.

She'd planned to avoid it, but her eyes went to the mirror automatically, for the check.

Thick stale-peach crust, the horrified grimace of a death mask setting in to her features underneath it. Eye-bags, with wobbly lines crayoned on top. Soft fat under her chin, hair-ends crackling out of warped, greasy waves. She turned and turned her head and could find nothing lovely about that face.

-It's just the light it's just the light, it's just the light-ing, she told herself, watched those clown-lips say.

*No wonder the gentleman doesn't want anything to do with you, eh? Look at you. Look at yourself, ya fuckin—*

—eh

　　　　—ah

—of course, his name wasn't really Glen. She'd looked him up online. He was a footballer, Spanish parents but raised here. Pictures of him began appearing in magazines she duly took out subscriptions to: hairgelled and sweaty at a couple of parties, herded out of nightclubs, clearly uneasy with the lenses trained on him and on the legs of last year's Miss Scotland (not that they'd ever really looked that happy together). He continued to ripple his torso, his beautiful arms, across hoardings, sun-drenched commercials and glossy centrefolds, though, pouting sensually over a variety of meat dishes. When the PR company who had birthed him announced they were replacing the kilt with more neutral clothes, so as not to alienate a London audience, the out-raged column inches had filled four whole A4 pages of her scrapbook.

She breathed out again, took him back with her across the floor.

That nasty wee smile to nowhere as she eased her hips back under the table, but she kept her head up this time.

Someone had topped up her wine. Not Chaals, presumably. The night off she could have been having, curled up with Glen and her fingers on the sofa, couple of bottles and the farm-sweet smell of herself.

She drained the whole glass. Fuckit.

- Now. *Chaals.* I presume you've made yourself familiar with the various packages we offer. So why don't you give me a little more of an idea of what I can do for you?

He didn't look up.

- Olivia, he said. I'm afraid I haven't been exactly honest with you.

The waiter made a soft noise in the back of his throat, and set their plates down. The steam rose; she could already taste the buttery richness of the port-spiked glazing.

- Thank you, she said, as the waiter shook out her napkin. You don't mind if I start?

A tense wave of the hand to say no, go ahead, and he tried again, as the first bite bloomed on her palette.

- I'm not. Not here to. Engage your services.

For fucksake, man, she thought. Your dinner's getting cold.

- I'm a. My name isn't. Not as such. I'm a journalist. I'm a journalist and my paper wanted me to. To write a piece about the. Experience. To. Yes.

She spoke through a mouthful, a plumply melting mouthful. She was fairly sure he wouldn't mind her manners now.

- I know who you are. You look a bit younger in your byline photo, mind. You've got a real trick with the words, Mr Mitchell. *Sandy.* I bet your friends at the council are delighted with you.

He looked at her properly, and she crammed another forkful in.

- This steak, by the way, is beautiful, and it's a really lovely choice of wine, too. You've got a talent for it. Now, are you wanting to ask me some questions, Sandy?

- I. Well. I suppose I just wanted to know why. You're a- You're well bred. You're clearly intelligent. You could be doing so many things with your life.

Keep smiling. Keep smiling.

- Mr Mitchell. I've read your columns. I know the kind of language you use. So let's stop pretending we're concerned about mah prospects here.

Slippage. Careful.

He hadn't touched a bite, just took another gulp of wine.

- All right. All right, he said. Perhaps I want to know *how* you can. You sit here and you look at me, as though. As though - with those damned moony eyes and all that - that - *suggestion* in your voice! And we both know you aren't interested in a single thing besides my wallet.

Across the restaurant, heads turned. She had a line ready for this.

- Mr Mitchell. I just provide a service that makes people feel a certain way about themselves -

Tiny drops of his spit hit her face as he hissed.

- Don't give me that bloody modern *feelgood* rubbish. What about the wives and families of the men whose money you're taking? What about your parents? Do they know how you degrade yourself?

She swept the last costly morsel round her plate to soak up the glaze, let it sink down into her before she answered him, topping up both their glasses as she went.

Keep smiling.

- No, darlin. It's only my company that's been paid for. You've not bought a right to those answers, cos you've not bought me.

A little flicker at his jaw, at that.

- If you'd wanted an interview, you should have asked for one. I'm only going to undertake the work I've been hired for.

She felt saliva rush to her mouth.

- We're in one of the best hotels in the country with an excellent bottle of wine to finish, you've hardly touched your duck, and the table beside us have just got some beautiful looking handmade chocolates with their coffee. If you'd like to sit here with me and enjoy these things, as we've already paid for them, perhaps I can help you to understand some of the reasons a client might feel the need to - work - with someone like me.

She let it rest there, on the table. Didn't force it with sauce or suggestion. This might, just might be done.

- I'm no here to be preached at, Mr Mitchell. You'll not convert me, so if we're going to end up at stalemate here, then I'll go and find myself alternative accommodation for the evening. And as I'm sure the agency made clear to your newspaper, while we always guarantee discretion, we have a no-refund policy. So. Sandy. *Mr Mitchell*. What's it to be?

———————————————

Sometimes, at work, she'd whisper to him, in her head. Isn't it a shame, Glen, that most Scottish men don't look like you?

He wouldn't ever say anything - that was the beauty of Glen, the silent beauty of him - but he'd stroke his hot bull breath into her neck like foreplay.

Behind the door, she heard noises; imagined him puttering in socks and boxers as she reclined, Glen grazing between her thighs. Almost shy when he stepped out, dropping the hotel bathrobe to reveal the pill already stiffening him. He had come prepared, she thought, how thorough, even as she yielded and flexed down for him, made her muscles small and tuned her brain away. But something sensual and rare was blooming and bursting, delicate, under her skin. Hypocrisy was such an aphrodisiac.

His fingers clawed at her haunches as he kept the rhythm up, cheered himself along with a muttered monologue.

- That's it.

That's it hoh yes that's it.

Take it.

Fucking take it.

Fucking take it, you whore.

From the pit of her stomach, Glen lowed, deep. She snorted, birled her head round flash-fast, and felt blood pool on her tongue as she sunk her teeth into the surprisingly toned, succulent flesh of his upper arm.

## She's Awfy No Well

### Nora Chassler

---

*Between friends nothing would seem stranger to me than true intimacy.*
- Ted Berrigan

Dear Pearl,

Please forgive me for everything I am about to say; I'm not on Prozac at the moment.

In case you don't know, this is what Selective Serotonin Reuptake Inhibitors are like: you're a kid again. You congeal in that vague confidence that comes from knowing you aren't a grown up yet, but that you will graduate. You're waiting, bored and confident. Unfortunately, Prozac does not induce those cool, trippy parts of childhood, where you imagine the courtyard behind your apartment building filled with lapping water, and how you'd jump out in an inner-tube and float by ninth storey windows, or dive down to fifth storey ones where - like you were in one of those fancy underwater tunnels in an aquarium - you'd stare into kitchens, at old ladies making lasagna, in curlers. You'd watch them as a shark. Then, needing air, you'd will away your weight, and rise back up into the reeling blue, to your sun-warmed waiting inner-tube, on top of New York City. You'd float, breathless, ecstatic... No, no, no, my old friend. Prozac is the long, low parts of being a kid where fuck all happens. You're watching reruns of sitcoms on the linty couch while trucks screech in the street and you flinch, but don't take your eyes off Jack Tripper. Prozac is profound ennui, tempered by the security of bizarre, nonsensical rules. Prozac is the hope - no, the certainty (because hope can have such complexities as doubt) of a future you will choose. The truth is nothing happens when you're on drugs. That's why folk take them.

You probably haven't gotten around to reading *Notes from Underground* yet? I gave it to you for your birthday sixteen years ago. That's OK.

In *Notes from Underground* the narrator begins: *I am a mean man. I am a miserable man. I think there is something wrong with my liver.*

I always thought that was funny.

I am miserable and there's gotta be something wrong with my liver by now. Because - this you'll remember - I've been drinking too much since we were fourteen. When I was fourteen, New Year's Eve - must have been, what? - 1986, I threw up a fifth of Jack Daniels on your motorcycle jacket in my mom's elevator. Sorry. Remember that sleazy middle-aged man got in and I said "Happy New Year!" and I gave him the finger? When you emailed me last week, you attached a photo someone posted of us on Facebook, two thirteen-year-olds at a party. I look like Billy Idol. Same haircut, same sneer. No, I'm not on Facebook. No, I don't want to be any-one's friend on Facebook. You think I'd see the fun in it! Boost (what is obviously) a fault in my confidence? I don't lack confidence (at least not in the way you think). I followed that 'get out there and sell yourself' advice for ten years, then quit. Actually that's a lie; I spent all my time beating myself up for not following it.

It's because I always have been miserable, Pearl; that's why you have been out of touch; I'm aware of that. Are you? I don't blame you. I really really don't. I mean, I'm such a narcissist; I'm convinced you got the idea to cut me out from me! I had just dropped another of our old friends. You were bewildered by the concept. By my lack of allegiance. I re-member the face you made over your tiramisu when I told you. Because me and this girl, "went way back." Like we were in the Craps or whatever that Irish gang is called in *West Side Story*. You used to love that movie. Anyway, next thing I know I'm adrift, Pearl-less. You never even replied to that pathetic postcard I sent from London about four years ago.

Well I got my comeuppance. For my sins I live in the city of D___. That's a quote from a Ted Berrigan poem, but the city in the real poem is New York. The poem goes: "For my sins I live in the city of New York / Whitman's city lived on in Melville's senses." I can't think of who to replace Whitman and Melville with for D___. Lenny and Carl from The Simpsons, maybe. There is something... *incomparable* about this place. As I write I see the sand-filled tin bucket in the car park in front of £-Stretcher that the checkout girls, in their tight-fitting polyester trousers, extinguish their cigarettes in. For some reason I just see it, not them, its tinyness there beside the gray roar of the dual carriageway. I also see the £-Stretcher sign. The week we moved here the plastic £-Stretcher sign fell off in a high wind and cracked; the next morning there were giant yellow splinters in the parking lot, the size of swords. For my daughters, this has the status of an event. We discuss and notice things. Anyway, it was immediately replaced with a banner; I thought it was temporary because they put it up all rumpled, like when you button a shirt wrong and it bunches. But it's still there, every morning on our way to school, the peek of its wrinkle waving meekly in the wind, as we wait for a break in the traffic, for our chance to cross the road.

Speaking of the color of Irn Bru and the feel of pies, the smell of petrol and the sugar high of 'tablet', of the mournful omnipresence of dreich - for these are the intersections of D___ and "the senses" - I should not be eating *this*: greasy, cold braised red cabbage, when my hands are frozen and itching, my skin peeling off. My eczema is getting worse and worse. I wear fingerless gloves all the time. My palms bleed. But here I stand, 9 a.m., shoveling it in, in front of the flame-effect gas fire. My neighbors garden rises out the window. Little sperm-like heads of snowdrops pierce his dirt. Why do his snowdrops grow? I spent forty quid at B&Q and nothing came up, not a bud could be bothered "twisting into itself". My garden has a rug of moss and weeds and weed grasses. I'm afraid to touch a thing. Sometimes I stand

out there crying at how little I understand: I know nothing
about how things grow and die. I don't believe what anyone
says either. I insist on relying *solely* on my own observations;
I want to watch the garden for a few years, and see what it
does. Speaking of nature, I just saw in the news - it was
one of the most emailed stories on the BBC website - that
some poor kid was killed by a komodo dragon. First time in
thirty years.

On the bottom of the page there was a link in "similar
stories" to one about an Orca at a "Sea Life Centre" that
thrashed and killed its trainer. In front of an audience. I love
that bit.  I mean, isn't it funny: every time a wild animal gets
a human it's on the news - it's *that* rare now. We were once
legit prey. Then we domesticated animals, settled down...
Which brings me back to gardens. No one we knew had one
in New York.  Only rich people had them. Even the poorest
people here get a strip of land in front of and behind their
homes. In New York you were lucky if you had a fire escape
to set your ashtray on. You had a wide ledge, though, Pearl.
That was quite cool. You had a nice view of rooftops and wa-
tertowers and if you leaned way the fuck out your bedroom
window you could see down to Riverside and across the
Hudson to NJ. My whole apartment faced a wall.

We used to live in a smaller town near here, me and
my kids. I liked it better. I walked them to school along a
wooded path, beside a burn. I thought the big horse chest-
nuts and limes shivered 'hi' when I jogged home under them.
They didn't like me much, those particular trees, but they
accepted me. Maybe it's just because they were younger
then, my kids; and the world seemed alive in that way it
does. Anyway, sometimes I stopped at the Botanic Garden
on the way home to our tiny freezing flat. I wandered between the red-leaved, foreign trees, avoiding their name-
plates, or did deep breathing in the heated, close green-
houses. I loved that little town and our cold flat and the
Botanic Garden.

Then I got a boyfriend - that's how I ended up here -
he believed that if you're miserable everywhere anyway, you

aren't entitled to a say in where you are. I did a chart for that. **A flow chart, no it was a pie chart, my fave.** Anyway this boyfriend, he convinced me to move to D___. Then we broke up, but I stayed. I didn't want to disrupt my kids' lives again so soon again.

To say I was taken in by this town's charms would be a massive exaggeration, but I did warm to the dilapidated grandeur. It seemed a good spot to drink myself to death. Like no one would notice, or give a fuck. No, not that they wouldn't give a fuck... that they would *understand*. Anyway I bet you didn't know it was the richest city in Europe from about 1880-1905. So we have a piece of this amazing old mansion. High ceilings, ornate mouldings, a view across the river. But outside our door it's pretty grim, Pearl. And my daughters' school looks like one of those temporary offices they build for foreman on construction sites. They have a permanent puddle, braceleted ( I know that's not a word, but this is a letter so I can write what the hell I want) with widely-spaced traffic cones, in front of the entrance. It's fun, actually; you get to watch parents' different ways of trying to keep toddlers from splashing in it.

*No one walks anywhere here* and I refuse to drive. I have this theory about being where you are, about how traveling makes you insensitive, about the merits of carrying yourself, but I can tell you later. My point is: we can walk the mile to school and not see a soul on foot. In bad weather the council clears the roads of ice, but not the pavement. All winter we risked it in the road. Sometimes we have to wait ten minutes to get across the dual carriageway. We watch the £-stretcher sign from the foot of the crosswalk. We stand there, beside the filthy road, it's usually raining or snowing, hoping someone will be bighearted enough to let us go. When I'm hungover I start to curse. "Fat fucking fuckhead drivers." The girls think it's funny. Once we've crossed, a bit further down the slope, we're wedged between the abandoned factories. They're nice. In London they'd have turned the old factories into flats or a museum or an arty cinema with a cafe selling vegan brownies. Here there's a halal butcher and a bathroom outfitters, if that's what you call it.

And of course it's always a shock when you do see the residents in the flesh, "outwith" their Meganes and Scenics, Astras, Audis and Puntos. Their fat middles are like huge innertubes, moving in that same way they do on a wobbly surface of water, independent of their owners.

Jesus, the only cheap foods to take away here are savory pies! The humanity. No Chinese lunch specials here, baby. No shrimp versus pork Hunan style with brown rice and a hot and sour soup. No sirree. I think the appeal of the pie is that it looks really neat. It can't be the taste: greasy gray flour. It's that the insides are enclosed, the mess of substance hidden, then they draw a cute little grid on top, for decoration. The Brits are obsessed with tidy uniformity. Plus they have very clear guidelines regarding what needs to be kept clean and what doesn't - what it's precious, *hubristic* even, to wash.

Maybe I need to start a new chart: what people wash here + explanations.

I do make charts - rather, I used to, until two months ago. You think I'm just throwing that in as a flourish. But I'm not kidding; I blu-tacked them inside the door of my press. (In Scotland a closet is usually called a press.) About a dozen Unabomberish illustrations on foolscap, filled in over the past year, since the move to D___. One shows hours worked per week. I do all the housework, obviously, or I did. I mean, I still do, but there is no one else here who might. I listed every task: take out all bins, change light bulbs, cook all food, shop, set up and dismantle Christmas trees, shop for birthday presents, decide what we eat, clean the toilets and tiles, pick up dirty cups, Hoover, dust, scrub the floors, wash the curtains, inside the kitchen cupboards, buy nit shampoo, doormats, notice when people have nits. One of the charts - a pie - successfully categorizes and quantifies "attentiveness", because housework can bleed into that (in my mind at least) and I wanted to make things clear. Another tries to tackle "being pleasant to loved ones." I'm really proud of these charts, Pearl. Because twice two **is** four, and it **is** relevant to being human, contrary to what Fyodor thinks. My ex thought I wasn't good at that last one, "being pleasant ..." - that's why I went on the Selective Serotonin Reuptake Inhibitors: because I was unpleasant to him and he hated to see me suffer.

The bar graphs are my best. Hours spent are simple, quantifiable. Twenty-five hours a week of housework, on average. Mostly in the evenings. Childcare has a different chart. Kids aren't housework. You've got to talk to them, read to them, watch the Simpsons with them and explain what things mean. Make sure they practice violin. You have to explain everything as best you can, so they don't turn out to be morons like everyone else. They're in school now, but I still "work" on them twenty hours a week. Obviously these overlap - I can shop with them sometimes, and help with their homework while I do the dishes, but you aren't allowed for there to be more than twenty-four hours in a day. Because jobs pay by the hour. Mine pays zilch! I get alimony and tax credits. He used to tell me to "bring something in". One day two months ago, I laid my charts out on the table, like a ship's Captain, I thought it would convince him, scientifically, that I wasn't worthless. "I don't want to get emotional about all this division of labour stuff. This is fact." I said. Or I didn't say it, but I hoped the serious look in my eyes conveyed it.

I barely saw the sole of his Rockports on the way out the door.

LOL. That reminds me of a time during your absence. I was in similar isolation. Living in London, around when I posted you that postcard. (I think it was a Paula Rego I got from an exhibit at a small museum.) My daughters and I spent the day in the park outside a cold crescent opposite Karl Marx's house. The door had one of those oval blue plaques on it. My eldest climbed a tree and I stood there for hours, waiting for her to get bored. She was about three. The other was just a suckling blob. I let her sister stay there in the black tree's armpit until it was dark. She sat in her nook, talking to herself, laughing, wringing her hands as part of some game she was making up. When she was done we just went home. The shop we were headed to was shut by then.

Should I be angry that you disappeared, especially when my father had just carked it? He'd been in my care for some time, you'll remember. Bah! Why take umbrage? I know for some people it's a relief, righteous indignation. For me it would be an *act*. Years ago, the second and last time a boy broke my heart I gave into it for about five minutes. My belief in my own goodness and purity was the motor of our persistent idiotic love. I should have just let it end; I did this time. See, Pearl: if I believe *I* have been wronged and you are the villain, that you left me like a fish plucked out of its bowl, that you "owe me", it somehow elevates us both; we're both now acting in that play that distracts us from who and where we really are. No one deserves to get off the hook that easy: to get to be the goody or the baddy. We're wretched little things creeping out of the sea, still, trying to make ourselves lofty. Our so-called "emotions" are no more than emergent fictions. I can't fit it all in here. It's not that complicated though, once you submit to the lingo...

Getting back to the subject of my dad dying: junkies are a great example of the lovestruck marginalized.

Ach I left that *all* out! Silly me! Forgive me, Pearl! I twatted on about the walk to school and how many dishes I do - like you care. I spilled some cabbage on the sheet I handwrote, and I thought I'd just leave it out; I thought it was this long thing about flowers and fake flowers and ebay and Moreno clowns and collectibles in general, and that guy on Bargain Hunt (my kids and me watch it fanatically on iPlayer) and how I wish I had a hobby... but *now* I can see it must have been this almost deep exegesis on junkies, because I can't find it on any of these sheets. I connected junkiedom to something about how outsider narratives don't work right. How when you have to be the sidekick or girl, the queer or the junkie, you have to take both sides, which strengthens the character but weakens the story. It made more sense the way I put it, but it's lost, alas.

My dad had figured out a way to be in the world; he was a junkie since he was twenty because he was a deeply spiritual soul in a time and place where God was not cool, where loving God was not an option. Think about it. What a lot junkies have! How they suffer! They're like fucking monks! Yes, really. You can't say they're any more delusional or any less selfless. Imagine devoting yourself so wholeheartedly and with such unwavering faith to a task, a job. It is their God. And they are Gnostics because they don't even claim to know God. They only *feel* him. Christ, I should not be eating day-old greasy cabbage while I get so worked up. I'll get terrible cramps. I'm sure there's a great Scots word for tummy cramps. *She's awfy no well! She's taken a turn...* Suffice to say junkies in Scotland are a whole other kettle of fish. It's passed on, generation to generation. Actually they had to blow up a tower block just to eradicate a few hundred of them. Well, not exactly, I mean you can't *eradicate* them, they are God's tribe, but they did blow it up and move them further afield. In NY when you think of junkie you think: I'll Be Your Mirror. Lou Reed. Lemme tell you: he would not have been a junkie here. Lou would have run a take-away menu distribution franchise and cheated on his wife with fat lasses in push-up bras.

Remember that other book I lent you, *Straw Dogs*, by John Gray? You probably didn't read it, that's cool. I'm no humanist. But what I think is - to love people is like a blanket. A very useful, manmade thing, love, like a blanket. "From each according to his ability, to each according to his need." That's what I think.

We Are All Equal in the Eyes of the Lord. That's what I fucking think.

LOL. Remember the day I got my eldest daughter baptized, "just in case"? Maybe that's what did it, maybe you just decided I was mad as a fish after that. I guess it was a bit weird for a Jew to hedge her bets by baptizing her daughter... but I figured, what if it *is* true? I didn't want to risk my darling girl heading straight to hell. (The irony is not lost on me.) Anyway, that night the wee one was about two months, and screaming her head off as usual. You said I should shut her in a room. I was mortified but didn't say anything; I strapped the baby to my chest and we left the house. Once out in the cold night she was asleep in moments, where she belonged, next to my heart and under my breath. Under street lamps.

Oh, sorry about *your* dad, by the way: that friend I cut off all those years ago emailed me about it. He should really have stopped with the Cuban fried chicken, the brisket on challah, the Marlboro Reds, the Coca-Cola. Maybe I should have mentioned that I knew he was dead in my text. Death and texts don't mix though, do they? Anyway. I remember once you were so pissed off at him you ran all the way down to Riverside Park, in a thunderstorm, to that leaf-clogged fountain that's a bald eagle over a giant open clam shell, at the bottom of 76th Street. I can see you there. Your arms spread, leaning over the clam basin, sobbing, your long soft mermaid hair quivering. I really wanted to make you feel better. I tried to make jokes. I tried to make light of it because that's what I do to myself. You wouldn't even take a hit of the jay I'd stolen from my ma, you were so mad.

I told the girls about that time he drove us all the way to Queens for the best icey in the five boroughs... I had the coconut even though they were famous for their lemon. We were taking the piss out of that Sting song that was a big hit that summer. "Pee Pee, let them Pee!" We were singing. In Ozone Park. With sticky hands.

I hope we'll have a nice time when you come next week. I already know what I'm gonna cook. Not cabbage, don't worry. I told the girls you're coming, they're very happy.

OK, Pearl. I have to walk the dog now, wait at £-Stretcher, get the kiddos. Come home and let them go on Club Penguin. (It's a "screen day" – computers, Nintendos, you name it, anything goes; tomorrow they get nothin' but books and baking with mad mom. I alternate: one day on, one day off. I try.)

I love it in D___ when it's sunny, that's the funny part.

I am so full *of* shit. I have these times when everything that I hear or see is totally meaningless, when I don't try to understand, and when I couldn't if I did. Like how in a dream there is no Universe. Do you know what I mean, Pearly? Both meaningless and all there is. I bet that's the way the world is to a baby. Maybe even to a tree! LOL.

Love,

    Sonia

## Here Wouldn't Be There

### Duncan McLean

---

The trouble with summer was the holidays. The hostel kids all came home to the island and hung about the street. So forty max was the best you could do for fear of flattening midge-crowds of them as they staggered about outside the chipper, making on massive drunkenness.

I went round the circuit again, getting a decent squeal out the tyres as I cornered the kirk, feeling my fingers buzz to numb as I battered down the long cobbled Strynd. Then in by the pierhead, where the kids were bugging around a really exciting moped so's I had to slow, swerve, and sink the foot along the front road before crossing the line at the lifeboat shed.

One minute twelve. Not bad considering.

The good thing with summer was the touroids. They stumbled about the island trying to appear human, giving the game away by looking at the wrong things, by looking wrong: dayglo fleecy jackets, hiking boots and rucksacks. We all wore tee shirts all summer, especially on foggy days.

I skited round the circuit again (one ten) then slipped in the touroid CD as I slowed down the Strynd slope. Across the road, staring at the ferry timetable on the pole, were two females of the species: brown legs, blonde hair, big back-packs. A typical touroid trait: just off the boat from the mainland, the first thing they do is work out how they're going to get back. Planning their escape. Some of us have been trying to work that out for twenty years.

The music kicked in: 'Dueling Banjos' out of *Deliverance,* manic twanging loud enough to rattle the wipers on the windscreen.

The touroids jumped, turned around, and I met them with a big grin and stary eyes. They looked worried, mut-

tered to each other, shifted the huge rucksacks. Then one
of them turned back to the timetable, while the other, jit-
teryer, looked up and down the street. That escape route
planning again! Maybe it was something you were born with
down there. Here it was the other way round: you knew from
birth there was no way out.  Or at least if you did get out
you could never come back here. Here wouldn't be there
any more.

The music started to speed up, and the jittery lass
looked over at me. I grinned wider, lolled my head over onto
my shoulder.

The jitter grabbed the other one by the elbow, gave
her a yark, and they headed off down the street, almost trot-
ting. It was a shame really, it really was: like shooting crabs
in a creel.

I took my foot off the brake and freewheeled down the
last of the brae, then turned and idled along the narrow
street after them. The banjos were going full volume, full
speed.  I crawled at their backs for a minute, watching the
way their thick socks rolled down over the tops of their
boots, making their legs look slimmer. I oozed up alongside,
then a little bit ahead, and stopped. I leant out of the window, crossed my eyes, and as they passed drawled out in my
best American hillbilly accent: 'Can I help y'all?'

The two of them paused, turned their faces slightly,
but didn't stop, edged past.

I inched on ten metres.  'Want a ride, ladies?' I said,
and crossed my eyes even harder.

They kept moving. 'No,' said the one at the front, the
timetable reader. 'No thank you. We're not going far.'

I nodded, blinked very slowly. 'Can I help y'all?' I said.

The jitter looked at me, and I saw her top lip curl back.
She turned to her friend.

'Get lost,' said the timetable-reader, and they squeezed
forward between my door mirror and the wall, their rucksacks scraping against the stone.  And off along the street
they trotted, thumbs under shoulder straps. They didn't look
back.

I was going to shout after them, ask them if they wanted a ride, but a movement in the rear-view caught my eye: another car trying to get along the street for God's sake: Piccadilly bloody Circus. So I headed up by the kirk and back round the front. One minute nine: excellent. 'Dueling Banjos' had finished.

At the pierhead again, I ejected the CD, and stuck it back in the door pocket between 'You Sexy Thing' out of *The Full Monty* (for outside the dances when cruising past the drunk-enough girls) and 'The Ride of the Valkyries' out of *Apocalypse Now* (for feeling like I was driving a na-palm-filled helicopter, all set to fly away from this place, torching it as I fled).

Up ahead, the shutters of the fish shop went down. A minute later, Kenny Hume backed out the door, plastic bag dangling from his wrist.

I tooted the horn, lifted a finger off the wheel at him when he looked over. He nodded, strolled across the street, leant his elbow on my mirror.

'What like?' he said.

'Bored to fuck.'

He shook his head. 'I've no time for that.'

'Too many fish to gut, Kenny?'

'Clams, boy, clams. Reckon old Guild's hit the biggest clam mine north of nowhere: surprised the Girl Mina wasn't couped over by the weight he brought home theday.'

I glanced out across the harbour. 'Want a lift?' I said.

He shrugged, went round the other side and got in.

'What you got in your carrier?' I asked.

'Ach, that's from Guild as well,' said Kenny. 'Supper.' He raxed around to drop the bag on the back seat.

I drove off, up round the kirk, down the Strynd, back to the pierhead, and over the line. One twenty.

'You're falling away,' said Kenny.

'These fucking schoolkids!'

'Aye. Still. Some of the girls, eh. Those sexy sixth years. Not bad!'

'Too young for the likes of us, Kenny.'

'Speak for yourself! Are you past it?'

'Not that. Just... I prefer a woman that's seen a wee bit of the world, ken.'

'Well *this* is a wee bit of the world.'

'A very wee bit!'

He laughed.

'Ken what I mean though,' I said. 'A lassie that's seen more than just here and the hostel on the mainland. That's been off and away... somewhere.'

'Dear oh dear,' he said, shaking his head. 'What are you going to do?  Talk to her?'

We both laughed, and I drove off: past the kirk, down the Strynd, then left at the bottom and away out of the village. As I cornered fast round the fifth green on the golf course road, there was a rustling from the back seat, then a faint clacking noise.

'What the fuck is in your bag?' I said.

'Ha! Lobster!'

I gave him a look.

'Guild was diving at the mouth-of-the-bay clambeds,' he said, 'And here was this lobster davering about, so...'

'He pocketed it.'

Kenny frowned. 'Are there pockets in a wetsuit?'

I snorted. 'Guild'll lift anything he finds down there: lumps of sea coal, starfish and sea urchins to dry out for the craft shop, drowned trawler-men's false teeth... lobsters out of someone else's creel.'

'Nah! Running wild it was,' said Kenny. 'He swore it. Turned out it was too small for the hotel to buy, so he just chucked it in with the clams. Quite right too. Ten dozen I bought off him theday.'

More clacking came from behind.

'Here,' I said, and slapped my hand on the wheel. 'We could cut its head off and send it away to my brother.'

He thought a sec, nodded. 'Not much of a trophy for your wall, a lobster's head, is it?'

'Fergus isn't going to stuff it,' I said, steering into the campsite. 'It's a wee bit of home from home, that's all.'

'Heard from him lately?'

'Aye: he texted last night, that's what put me in mind of it. Wanted to know how my collection of skulls was getting on.'

I pulled up by Kenny's caravan. With the engine off, you could hear the lobster stirring in the bag.

'And?'

'Well, I buried them in the garden, so the worms would eat the flesh away, but now I can't remember where I put the bloody things! By the time I find them it'll be Christmas, and he'll be back, he won't need minding of home sweet home.'

We got out. The beastie in the bag fell silent as he carried it across the grass and up the rickety steps. Maybe the swinging motion reminded it of the undersea eddies. We went in.

Kenny lifted the carrier onto the draining board by his wee sink and looked at it sitting there, wee juts of angular body pressing against the plastic.

'Are you not going to let it out?' I asked. 'Give it a basin of water to swim about in or something?'

He shook his head. 'Last thing it needs now's water. It'd drown in seconds flat.'

'Eh?'

'Tap water - worse than air, so it is. They drown in anything but sea.'

'Tough. How about lager?'

'Never tried that.'

'Shite Kenny. I've seen you try it a million times.'

'Not on a lobster, smartarse. You'd need a lot of tins to cover the bastard over. And what a waste if it didn't like it.'

'Did they teach you nothing at fishmonger's academy?'

He pinched the bottom seam of the placcy bag between finger and thumb, and slowly pulled it up and off to the side.

There was a thrashing and a clacking, then a wee thud as the lobster landed on the metal sinkside amongst the dirty dishes and beer cans.

'Christ that's a bluey!' I said.

'They're always blue,' he said. 'They've got the blues.'

And he launched into singing:

*'Well I woke up this morning*
*Sea all around my bed*
*Conger ate my baby*
*Lord I wish I was dead...'*

I bent over to look at the beast. 'Who put the rubber bands round its claws?'

'That would've been Guild. They'll take a finger off if they get hold of one. Nippy!'

As he spoke, the lobster slumped, clattered into a bowl with its tail, knocking it over and sending fragments of cornflake and dribbles of milk flying all over its smooth blue back.

'Look at that,' I said. 'It's gone and fell down, and we never even knew it was standing up. A great feat of strength for a crustacean, and no bastard even noticed!'

'It's hard being a shellfish out of water,' said Kenny. 'Ask Fergus.'

'Exactly: Glasgow, it's a different world.'

He stepped to the wee two-ring stove, and tipped open the lid of the big soup pot that was sitting there. He sniffed, then keeked inside.

'Can't believe it,' he said. 'It's clean. Right: action. You take this, I'll take the fucking beastie, and we'll away down the shore and get some water to cook it in.'

'Christ, have you not got a tap in here?'

'Ach, trust me Alistair, this is the way with the denizens of the deep: stick them in seawater, bring it to the boil, then eat. That's all you need. Brings the flavour out like nothing else.'

He thrust the pot against my chest, reached over and grabbed the lobster round the middle like a packet of biscuits, then leapt out the door and danced away through the other caravans, waving the thing over his head and singing to it as he went.

I followed, laughing and shaking my head.

We went in and out of the tents towards the sea, stepping over the strings pegged into the turf, making detours around bottle-gas stoves with pans of beans bubbling. A couple of the campers looked weirdly at us, but we never minded. I started beating out a bit of a rhythm on the bottom of the big pot as we strode along, and Kenny waggled the lobster in the face of two wee kids playing in the dirt, and they screamed and laughed.

He led the way through the gate and down the bit of path onto the rocky shore. Away to the right were the stone piers of the village, and off left the salmon cages under the slopes of the hills, then the narrow mouth of the bay and the ocean beyond.

'Here, I was just thinking,' I said. 'Where's the fucking sewage outfall from the campsite bogs?'

'Relax,' he replied. 'The tide's flowing out: we're upstream of the campsite pipes.'

'Thank God for that.'

'Right enough, we are downstream of the village outfall.'

'God's sake!'

'Tell you what, we can sieve the water when we get back to the caravan.' He lifted the lobster up to face him. 'Don't you worry my friend. We wouldn't boil you to death in unsanitary conditions.'

The lobster waved its claws about in a feeble way, and Kenny laughed. Then he stopped. Down at the water's edge, kneeling on the pebbly beach with their backs to us, so their denim backsides were bobbing up in the air, were the two blonde touroids from earlier.

'Jesus Christ,' said Kenny. 'What a sight.'

'I ken this pair,' I said. 'I offered them a lift earlier and they knocked me back. You do your best for island hospitality, but...'

'I'd do my best for them, I tell you. Blondes! Are they Swedish or something?'

'Nah, sounded more like Scottish to me. I'm no expert though.'

'Scottish? Ah well, you can't have everything. They're fucking stunners, though, eh.'

'I suppose so. I never noticed.'

'You never noticed! What's the matter with you?'

'Ach, just more touroids,' I said, but too loudly, so one of the lassies heard and turned round.

'Help us,' she said. 'This bird...'

We glanced at each other, stepped forward and crouched down beside them: Kenny inbetween and me off the jitter. I set the pot down on the ground, base up, and sat on it.

'It's a heron,' said Kenny.

'It's dead,' I said.

The timetable-reader puffed out a little gasp of breath.

'Is it definitely dead?' she said.

'Aye, definitely,' I said. The feathers were lying wrong, looking ruffled, not all tucked in like they should've been.

'Look at that round its legs,' I said, and pointed at the orange net-twine tangled amongst its spindly shanks. 'It'll have stepped in that out in the shallows, hunting, and got twisted up and tripped. And drowned. Spends all its life standing around in the water but drowns in two inches of it!'

'We thought we saw it move,' said the jitter.

'We came to look at the view then we saw it lying here. But we thought the wings were kind of struggling a little bit.'

Kenny nudged the bird's body with the front end of the lobster. It didn't react.

'Nope,' he said. 'Not long gone, but gone.'

'It's beautiful,' said the timetable-reader.

Before I'd just seen the touroid getup, but now I saw her face. Some words came in to my head but I didn't say them out loud. Instead I went; 'See when I was a boy? I always thought a heron would make a right good weapon.'

The two lassies looked at me, frowning. Blonde eyebrows.

'Look at that beak,' I said, pointing. 'Long and pointy and sharp as a razor for stabbing fish. And then the long neck and the long body and the long legs. Imagine rigor mortis had set in, right, the bird all stretched out in a straight line - well, you'd be able to pick it up by the ankles, wouldn't you. Then - whu! whu! whu!' I mimed whirling the thing about my head. 'You go steaming in to the opposition. Pin point accuracy and lethal effect.'

'That's ridiculous,' said the jitter.

'That's gross,' said the other.

'You could take somebody's eye out with that,' said Kenny.

'I never actually done it,' I said, 'It's just one of those daft things that comes into your...'

'Wait,' said the jitter, lowering her hand from her mouth where she'd clapped it. 'I know you: you're the twat that followed us down the street just after we'd got off the ferry.'

'What? Me? No!'

'Jackie, look at him!'

The reader, Jackie, looked me up and down.

'I've just come off work,' I said. 'I never followed no one.'

'You look just like him,' said the jitter.

'Weren't his eyes a bit funny?' said Jackie.

'Ah ha!' I slapped my hands on the sides of the pot. 'Yes!  That was my brother.'

They looked at me.

'My brother, Fergus. When you mentioned the crossed eyes: give-away.  I blame the inbreeding. Either that or he got hit by a heron at an early age, eh!'

They didn't laugh.

'That'll be him all right,' I went on. 'What an embarrassment!  Did he get his banjo out?'

They looked at me.

'He's at the uni in Glasgow studying... eh... banjo.  But now he's back for his holidays and...'

'Listen,' said Kenny, and they turned away from me and my beamer, thank Christ. 'I've been thinking. The problem with your theory, Alistair, is the legs.'

'What theory?' I said.

'The first time you hit some poor bastard with your heron,' he went on, 'The legs would just snap off.'

'Forget it,' I said.

'Look at them,' he said. 'Two bits of scaly spaghetti. You'd have to strengthen them somehow, ken: tape a metal rod up each leg and together at the bottom or something, give yourself a bit of strength. Or one rod - up its arse I suppose.'

'Aye, very funny Kenny. Drop it though, eh?'

'Of course, the problem then'd be you'd be drawing attention to yourself. Everyone would see you were up to something. The beauty about walking around with a heron is it's a natural object, so no one suspects nothing. But once you start tampering with it... the game's a bogey.'

'Are you being serious?' the jitter asked Kenny.

'Like hedgehogs,' he said. 'If you were using them as some kind of throwing weapon, like a ninja star, fine. You could walk about with a bag of them and no one could say nothing. But once you start filing their spikes to points, or gluing broken glass down their backs, well, bang goes your cover, ken what I mean? Or a swordfish...'

'Oh my God!' shouted the jitter. 'Is that a real lobster?'

In all the excitement with the dead bird, I'd forgotten why we came to the shore in the first place. Kenny had laid his supper down on the sand, and it was moving in a very very slow trembling kind of scuttle towards the sea.

He leant over and picked the beast up, and held it out to the lassies. They yelled, and leapt to their feet.

'They're crazy!' cried Jackie. 'They're all crazy here!'

They started backing away from us.

I scrambled to my feet, put myself between them and the lobster. 'No no!' I said. 'It was just a joke.'

'So why the hell are you walking about waving live things with claws in people's faces?' said Jackie.

'Eh... we were just about to liberate it,' I said. 'Return it to the wild. Isn't that right Kenny?'

He hadn't got up, but was bent over the heron, stroking its feathers. 'What?' he said.

'The bastard fishmonger had it sitting in his window - alive! - and me and Kenny went past and thought, jeez, the cruelty of that! So we went into the shop, and I distracted the guy by pretending to want ten dozen clams, while Kenny grabbed the poor old lobster, stuffed it up his jumper, and made a break for it.'

'Bonny bird,' said Kenny, and started crooning.

They looked at him, moved another inch backwards.

'Don't go,' I said. 'We were just coming down here to put it back in the sea, to give it its freedom.'

'I find that hard to believe,' said the jitter, taking another step back.

'Stay!' I said. 'Christ, don't go! Look, you can help do it if you like.' I reached down and grabbed the lobster. It was cool and dry, and didn't struggle. 'Here,' I said. 'Let's set it free. Come on.'

I stepped back towards the sound of the water, beckoning them with one hand while waving the lobster seawards with the other. I raised my eyebrows, gave a wee smile, and took another step. Now the lassies started to come after me.

'That's the job,' I said, and turned to walk down the last shelf of beach to where the waves lapped. I knelt down on the damp sand there, and waited till they arrived. The jitter stayed standing, a pace off to the side, but Jackie hunkered down beside me. 'Do you want to do it?' I said.

'No,' said the jitter.

'You,' said Jackie.

Holding the lobster in both hands, I lowered it down till it was resting on the surface of the water. Then I pushed it outwards, launching it out into the bay like a model boat. My wrists dripped as I lifted my hands high. The lobster floated away from the shore in the gentle current, and Jackie reached out and patted me on the back. I shivered.

We watched. For half a minute the lobster drifted away from the shore, then it flipped over and headed, belly up, for the campsite sewage outlet just down the coast.

'Is it all right?' said the jitter.

'It's in heaven,' I said. 'Look how relaxed it is.' Something orange winked at me from a wavetop: the rubber bands round the pincers. I coughed. 'Aye, it's fine.'

'Are you sure?' said Jackie.

'Lobsters always swim like that, didn't you ken?' I watched it go. 'It'll wait till it gets close to its, eh, burrow, and then it'll dive down.'

'I'm glad it's all right,' said the jitter.

'It's good to feel you've done something useful with your day,' said Jackie.

I stood up, stretched my arms out wide to take in the whole sweep of the bay.

'Island life,' I said. 'It can be dull sometimes for a restless intellect such as my own. But one certainly does come to appreciate the beauties of nature. And realise one's place in the fragile ecosystem that...'

I trailed off, distracted by grunts and crunches from where Kenny was crouched.

Jackie looked up, smiled at me. 'Have you always lived here?'

'Where else is there?' I said loudly, and laughed. 'I'll show you everything.'

'Come on you bastard!' shouted Kenny, and there was a loud clunk: stone on stone.

The three of us turned away from the view and back towards Kenny. He had moved a flat slab under the heron's neck, and was cracking down on it, two handed, with a sharp-edged beach stone.

The jitter sucked breath in through her teeth.

'Nearly got it,' said Kenny, and brought the stone crashing down again. There was the sound of splintering bone, a few feathers flew up in the air, and Kenny shouted in triumph.

'Ah ha!' he cried, grabbing something up, and jumping to his feet. He turned towards us, eyes gleaming. Spread across his blood encrusted palms was the long-beaked head of the heron, and a couple inches of its floppy neck.

'One more for your collection,' he said.

## Celebrity Gossip

## Alan Bissett

---

'Let me tell you something,' John said, pointing at the rows of raised, semi-dazed faces, at gel-spiked hair and hooped earrings and the chewing-gum motion of their mouths. 'I know I just look like a suit to you, and fair enough. You're right to be suspicious of men in suits. There are too many of them in London, where I live now.'

Stop. Switch index cards. From *1/ SUITS IN LONDON* to *2/ SKOOSH!*

'But I'm not one of them. I've never been one of them. I'm one of you.'

The boys at the front, nipping each other like warring insects, were struck by the glare from a teacher at the side of the hall. John coughed, let things settle before the next plink and fizz.

'When I was at this school – in the pre-internet dark age of the early Nineties – I edited the school magazine, the charmingly titled *Skoosh!* The most popular section was "Behind the Blackboard", where I made jokes about the teachers, harmless wee stories imagining their lives at home.' John shifted into a Yank accent, a TV presenter's cocked stance. "Miss Dreever's got her kids well trained: ten press-ups and cold showers if they don't finish their All-Bran!" He raised an accented eyebrow. "Does Meezes Sutherland like it when Meezter Sutherland talks zee French to her?"'

Oooohs curled out across the hall. John laughed.

'A couple of them were kinda close to the edge. And not all of the teachers, uh, took it on the chin.' He sniffed, tapped his cards. 'Well, my job is pretty much the same as it was then. It's just that the people I write about now are a bit less... local.'

A burble of acknowledgement travelled the hall and

the teachers flashed smiles. Card 2, *SKOOSH*, was slipped to the bottom of the stack as Card 3, *DRUMGAVEL EXPRESS*, whispered its entrance.

'I did my school work experience at *The Drumgavel Express*, but knew I wanted something more. I needed to be something... bigger.'

There was a layered silence now. They'd all stopped fidgeting, even the boys in the front row who'd stared neutrally as John had stepped onstage, the way dogs regard a stranger passing them in the street.

'Show you what I mean. Bit of Philosophy for you.' He began conjuring with his hands for them. 'A wooden ship leaves a harbour to go across the world. As the journey progresses, each plank on the ship is replaced. At each dock, some of the crew leave, some arrive, so that by the time it docks at its final port, there isn't a single crew-member or plank left that was part of the original ship.'

John paused.

'Is it still the same boat? Who thinks it is?'

A couple of hands went up.

'Who thinks it isn't?'

A forest of them.

*Groups are drawn towards the most immediate power source. If only a few say yes to the first notion, dubiety is established. When the second is put forth, people vote with the confidence that they're in a majority.*

John said, 'Really?' and watched the word make the hands curdle like weedkiller. 'What makes you sure it isn't? Did you know that all of the cells in your body completely replace themselves every few months? There isn't a single cell in you now that existed when you were born. But you're still the same person, right?'

The kids tutted at each other. *Course it's the same boat! I wis only pittin ma hand up cos they were! See youse!*

'Memory makes us who we are. Our link to the past. That's why, even if it's a different building, this is the same Drumgavel High.'

He gestured to an assembly-hall so new he could smell

the fresh, institutional green of the paint, and regarded the pupils evenly. The familiarity of the blazers bloomed in him for a second, a dislocation as he realised he wasn't

gaz mcallister

*ya stupit wee*

       look i never popped a stiffy in the shower

The blazers were still now.  Listening.

John pressed the lectern with his hands and leaned forwards.

'And also why, seventeen years later, I'm still just the former editor of the school magazine.'

When he'd told Gwen about the email from the Rector, she'd lifted her eyebrows, placed down her wine glass, and he'd sensed a pitch.  'I know what you're going to say, John, but think about it.  Boy from deprived area makes good. Bullied.  Overcame the odds.  The girls could interview you about celebrity encounters?'

He'd carried on twirling the noodles round his fork.

'Perfect for a documentary on that commercial channel up there, John.  What's it called?' Gwen pointed a forked prawn.  'Give you some telly profile too.  Print media is dying on its arse.  You need to think about a career beyond the column.'

John downed his Chablis then refilled it.

On his walk through Drumgavel, he cut a simple, clean figure, taking nothing with him except the numbered index-cards pressed into his suit pocket.  There was certainly no camera crew in attendance. No ceremony. He hadn't even wanted to take a taxi from the train station, had trusted his feet, following the old route, just to feel it properly, be part of its warp and weft again.  Through the lanes and past the library: taking his time, as the dog trail of it opened around him.  There was still a queue beyond the bakery, sniffing along the promise of a warm pie, but it was Greggs not Allardyce & Sons.  The High Street felt hollowed out now. Bumps-a-Daisy: *CLOSED*. Carla's Gladrags: *CLOSED*. Rosetti's: *CLOSED*. Inglis Bookshop, where Sun Tzu's *The Art of War* had opened a chest of glowing weapons to him: *CLOSED*. The laundrette his mum had worked in, while John sat on a spinning machine, listening to them gossip about Senga's man's mistress and Linda's drinking and Denise's eldest yin's weight gain.

CLOSED

Tesco. Ladbrokes. McDonalds.

Kids stamped and grabbed at each other. He strode through the lunchtime mass, their jacket-crush, their fat noise. Hunger made them scrappy – they leapt, boxed in and out of doorways. Shoppers navigated the thick spillage of them, until a lanky woman with a buggy barked, 'Oot ma road!' and cut through their floe. The boys settled back behind her, watched her charge down the High Street, then sniggered and went back to their pies.

The new building sat among the suburbs like a space colony, all proud with glass and steel. That style had once meant cutting-edge in London, but now, in a recession, simply meant pricey greenhouse and fearful staff wondering if the money spent on fuschias in the lobby could've saved Tom from Accounts. Sun reflected off the school, making John shade his eyes with his index-cards. Summer was winding down; the term was winding up. Boys chased a ball across the playground, a mad train of them, which he stood and watched for a while. Their shouts coated each other. Lads chased and scrabbled. Girls drifted across the pitch, giddy with mischief, raising hands in front of someone shying the ball, until the boys chased them and the girls chucked only-a-game comments behind themselves like empty crisp-packets.

John was soon lulled by the familiar pattern of it, the manic action: the ball moves and power flows round it. Boys jostle to be closest, dictate its direction, and the most harassed lash out against pushing jackets. In the absence of a referee, the game just shifts to those ruthless enough to take charge.

He peeled away towards the school entrance, straight into a startled kid. The index cards flew from John's hands. 'Oops,' he said and the kid grunted at him, then bent and helped John retrieve the cards. 'Thanks,' John said and the kid mumbled, 'Sawright,' and the two of them crouched for a few seconds, picking at the ground like a farmer and his son searching out the first buds of Spring.

The Rector met him in the lobby, shook his hand firmly and said, 'Mr Clayton, we meet at last. Hope there are no paparazzi with you!' He mimed a check over each shoulder. It was a joke so familiar it made John's teeth hurt. But the smile did its work.

'Not this time.

The Rector laughed.

Soon he was showing John round the new school, flicking a wrist towards gleaming, hi-tech smart boards, an actual gymnasium with running-machines, and a canteen which resembled an American milkshake bar. John 'wowed' in the right places, congratulated the Rector as though he were complimenting the new extension to his home, remembered chalk dust, wooden monkey-rungs, skinny formica tables, the smell of cabbage and industrial bleach. The smokey fug of the bogs. He couldn't get used to the sight of blue blazers floating through these futuristic corridors.

Eventually John said, 'Where did the money come from for the new school?'

The Rector stopped walking.

'Public-private partnership. One of New Labour's better innovations.'

John nodded. 'Ah, one of them.'

The Rector narrowed his eyes then smiled. 'Shall we continue?'

'Sure.'

He pressed on a door, behind which John half-expected to see a team of robots, then patted John into the room. 'I wasn't here when you were a pupil, but some of the old staff do remain. They're very much looking forward to seeing you again.' John felt himself being shepherded round the room, powerless to resist the battery of familiar faces which rose from the past before him. Twice the Rector introduced him to someone with the comment, 'Better be careful what you say...' Another old one. At least it allowed him to lower his voice, lean in and say, 'Why, what do you know?' then warm himself in the gentle mirth that followed.

Mr Connolly, Modern Studies, his big welcoming Drumgavel palm. Mrs Harris's wee bird-like wrists and shaking beads. Mrs Baird, his old art teacher, grown even hippier and When I'm Old I Shall Wear Purple-ish. 'Know whit I mind about you?' she was saying, her breath clambering up towards him, 'You, John Clayton, always used to compliment my dress sense. Just a brooch or a scarf or something. It felt genuine.'

'Did it really?'

She hooted. 'Far cry from now eh?'

John opened his mouth then closed it again. 'Lovely school,' he said, 'How are you finding it?'

Mrs Baird scrunched her face up and leaned in. 'It's hopeless, John. Knocked up wi a bittay plaster and spit.'

'Looks alright to me.'

'It's a bloody rip-off.' She took John's hand, led him into a corner, and he felt his pulse quicken. He knew these moments, harvested them at parties, when someone, having grown too bold on bubbly or powder, would decide to settle an old score with a nod towards a draped exit. So what's the word from the set? A cheating boyfriend? A bulimic girl-friend? Look as though another bright new star could burn out early? Delicious as following a trail of sweets. It was the Scottish thing they trusted; he was never slow to play up his roots, hearing some milk-white starlet drawl across a Mojito, 'God, what must that place have been like for you?' before he practised a pained face.

But Mrs Baird's gossip was a little more prosaic than he was used to.

'A private company builds the school and "lets" it to the local authority. Can ye imagine? Havin tae pay rent on a *state* school to a private company? And to keep their costs low, the company knock up any auld pish.' She thumped a wall. It made an unexpectedly hollow sound. 'I could just about put ma fist through that. The fitba pitch is the wrang size.  Half the so-called smart boards dinnay even work.'

John raised an eyebrow.  'Sounds like my office.'

Mrs Baird folded her arms.  'Don't geez it.  You're no gonnay invite Cheryl Cole round then make her sit on a milk crate.'

'You got me,' he smiled.  He swayed from side to side and wrung his hands.  She didn't say anything, just blinked at him, and he upped the wattage of his smile.  'My place is great for parties.'

Mrs Baird nodded.  'Ye awright there, John?'

He stopped swaying.  'Yeah.  Course.  What do you mean?'

'Nothing.  Forget I asked.'

'Sure,' John said.

There was some sort of fly buzzing through the conversation that he couldn't quite snatch.

'You've probably just had too much coffee.'

He rubbed his nose.  'Listen,' he said, 'What about Mrs Thompson?  Is she still here?'

Mrs Baird sighed.  'Dee passed away, John.'

'*No.*'

'I'm afraid so.  Took a heart attack in frontay the class wan day.'

'God, did she really?'

'It was in aw the papers.  Well, the Scottish ones anyway. Might no have reached you doon there.'

'When was this?'

'Uh... let me think.  February 2006.'

Valentine's Catfight! **JEN**: I want my husband back! **ANGELINA**: Hands off!

'That's terrible.'

'Aye,' said Mrs Baird, 'She spoke very highly of you. "One of the most talented pupils I ever had," she said. "Knew he'd go far."'

'Dee Thompson told you that?'

'Many times.'

---

His next stop was the library, for an interview with the

current editor of the school magazine. The library, of course, was all white walls and screens, more like the office space of an internet company than the brown, stained room of his memory, in which a solitary spider plant crept with Amazonian mystique. As he approached her table, the girl stood quickly, and when he shook her hand she almost whispered the name 'Kerry Wright'.

'Pleased to meet you, Kerry. John Clayton.'

'Aye,' she said, 'I know,' and blushed a little.

They seated themselves next to a bank of graphic novels and John unloosened his tie. The shuttle round the school had caused a light sweat.

'She's been called the next John Clayton,' the Rector said, 'Mainly by me.'

Kerry held her head and went, '*Waaargh.* Never sure if it's a compliment or not.'

John pulled at the cuffs of his shirt, looked up at the Rector. The Rector's smile seemed to explode. 'It's a compliment, Kerry.'

'Glad to hear it!' she laughed, then pointed to the teapot and lifted her brow at him.

'Please.'

The Rector excused himself, and Kerry tracked his progress to the door. As soon as she heard the soft click, her mouth opened and words flew out at John: 'This isnay part of the interview, but I just wantay say it's like a *total* inspiration to meet a famous newspaper columnist. That someone who went to Drumgavel High could be that? Well. That is just so excitin tay me.'

'Thank you,' John said, which every book on conversational skills agreed was how to best respond to praise.

She fumbled with the dictaphone. 'I can never get this thing tay work. Hang on. Is that light on?'

'No.'

She shook it. She blew on it. 'Och, I'll just write,' she said, 'Sorry about that.'

'It's fine,' he said, 'It's your interview. I won't talk too fast, okay?'

'Aw cheers. Bet this didnay happen when you were editor ay the school mag.'

'Are you kidding. My issue was banned. I was nearly expelled.'

'Really?' Kerry gasped, 'Why?'

'I implied that the Rector's home-life was... shared by another man.'

She leaned forwards. 'Seriously? Was he gay?'

John shrugged. 'Didn't expect anyone to take it to heart.'

'Wow,' she said, 'How cool. I hope they ban ma issue. You make sure ye give me some good stuff in the interview then.'

He chuckled gently. 'I'll try my best.'

'Right,' she said, putting her pen to the notepad with a flourish. They both smiled at some absurdity. 'First question. Are you ready, Mr Clayton?'

'I'm quite ready, Kerry.'

'Good. So, what do ye think ay the new building?'

---

The interview ambled through predictably adolescent territory: What were you like as a teenager? Who were your favourite bands? Did you ever sing the school song? Each time, John was careful to give at least one quote-worthy chunk of copy, laced with wit, that she could blow up beside his picture. He paced his answers so Kerry could write it all down. When he told her about the bullying, she tutted on his behalf and her face softened.

'Aye,' she said, 'Ma third year was really tough too.'

When she asked about his job, and the celebrity names began to blossom from his replies, he'd see her write faster and underline things. She nodded, laughed and cooed, and he could imagine her in ten years, working the parties, armed with irony and flattering the stars. It was endearing, this early schoolgirl version, the gaze intensifying and pen wagging when the topic of a recent scandal about a footballer arose.

'You're doing really well,' John said, breaking off a story to make her raise her head, startled.

'Thank you,' she said.

'Is this your ambition then? To write for a national newspaper?'

Kerry flattened her pen to the pad and leaned forwards. 'Well, let's just say that I dinnay want tae hang about in Drumgavel the rest ay ma life.'

'Good answer,' he grinned, 'Not enough people in this town with ambition.'

She tapped the rings of her notepad and looked down her questions.

'Just a couple more, if that's awright?'

'Go for it.'

'Right,' she said, and took an intake of breath. 'Do ye think it's fair that the paparazzi stalk and harass celebrities?'

John sipped from his mug and looked at her over the rim. Then he set the mug down.

'Well,' he said, 'No. Sometimes they can go about things too aggressively. But at the same time, there's a public appetite for those photos. Otherwise, why would people buy the papers?'

She moved her shoulders. Shards of something in her eyes. 'For news?'

'Didn't you just *ask* me about a whole load of celebs?'

'Naw. You telt me about them.'

'People...' – he said, searching the text of an opinion piece by one of his colleagues – 'live in fragmented communities these days. This is how we bond with each other, through the stories of famous people we feel like we know. A sort of virtual community, if you like.' Then he opened his hands and laughed. 'Is this really stuff which kids want to hear about? Wouldn't you be better running something about the *Twilight* films?'

Kerry mused on this, turning a slow circle with her pen in the air. 'Young people might be interested to know why the media sneers at women's body shapes. That's some-thin' which affects girls oor age.'

John ground his teeth.

'You have to remember, Kerry, those women want to be famous. They use the media when it suits them. They need us to give them publicity, so they must accept that that makes them fair game.'

Kerry tapped her pen on her hand. She wasn't even writing these answers down now. 'Did you no once claim ye'd studied Philosophy?'

'I didn't "claim" to,' he said, 'I did study it.'

'Aye,' she said, 'That's whit I mean.'

*Stepping into that lecture hall in St Andrews, into a room full of people who instantly seemed cleaner, sleeker, brighter than him. He made wee crab-like steps to a seat, through the smooth, blonde chatter of their accents. Naw, Johnny. Ye're as guid as any ay them. Bring it oan. The lecturer entered the hall, his clothes almost at one with the architecture, arranged his papers, stared at his audience and then released it: 'All philosophy is the gradual coming to terms with your own death.'*

'So, Mr Clayton, who's yer favourite philosopher?'

John stared at Kerry for a few seconds. She sat there, biting her pen and nodding for him to answer.

Eventually he managed to say: 'Dumbledore.'

She raised a sharp eyebrow, wrote it down. 'Good answer.'

'Thank you.'

---

The assembly hall just felt too new. It seemed sentient, a giant artificial intelligence housing them all. There was the Drumgavel High crest on the wooden standard at the back, the Dux medal winners engraved immortally, but it was a museum piece in this gleaming space, with its silver spotlights and computerised screen showing school news items.

John searched across the rows, but couldn't spot her. Their interview over, Kerry had merged back into the body of the school they same way he floated invisibly through parties, listening. 'The Cocktail Ninja,' his colleagues had once dubbed him. John coughed: it made a square echo in the hall. He shifted his stance a little, leaned into the mic, changed index-cards.

*5 / PERIANDER*

'Let me tell you about another philosopher,' John said, 'Periander. No, it's not a mineral water. Died in 588 BC. Know how he died?'

He hoped Kerry had her notebook out for this bit.

'Never mind your Heath Ledgers or Michael Jacksons. Wanna hear about someone who went out in *style?*'

A couple of the kids nodded eagerly.

'He instructed two young men to meet a third at a designated place, then kill and bury him. He arranged for four young men to hunt those two down, then kill and bury them. He arranged for a larger group of men to hunt down the four, then kill and bury them. Having made all these preparations, he went out to meet the first two young men. For he – Periander – would be the first killed.'

The boys in the front row squirmed with shoot-em-up excitement at how goddam cold that was. But most of the others were frowning. Some of the teachers lining the side of the hall leaned forwards, chins in hands. He'd actually forgotten what the message behind this story was. Trust no-one? Life is fleeting? Be a badass?

'Can you imagine that?' John said (if you forget your place, simply talk conversationally to your audience, keeping them at ease), 'You're in that group of young men, and don't know if someone's going to be coming after you? Isn't that chilling?'

He glanced at the next index card, which read *11 / MEETING LADY GAGA*. But he'd just done 5 /. The card after that was *8 / BE ALL YOU CAN BE*.

A slow curl in his gut. No.

*7 / DEFYING THE ODDS*

*9 / BRITAIN'S GOT TALENT*

*10 / BE YOUR OWN BRAND*

He tried to shuffle the cards as the hall enlarged

around him. His hands fumbled. 'So you just, uh, give me a moment here and think some more about, uh, Periander's death.'

John was keenly aware of them all listening now, and their many eyes, the whispers that had started sneaking through the assembly hall. One of the kids shouted from the back. A few others laughed.

'What was that?' John said, peering through the lights.

The kid repeated it, made a weight of mirth in the crowd around him. A teacher rushed to the boy. 'Aye, well,' John said, 'I'm the wan staunin up here, mate, no you.'

There was a rumble in the hall. He saw a teacher fold her arms. The cards danced in his hands.

It was then that he spotted Kerry in the second row, dictaphone out and the red light glowing. The girl next to her murmured something and Kerry nodded, staring at John.

He placed his cards down on the lectern, looked into darkness. The hall waited. But when he opened his mouth to speak, nothing came out. He rubbed his nose and tried again, but nothing came out.

## The Astronaut

## Jason Donald

---

It's not the face you imagined you would end up with. A plate face with a double chin. All the parts are present and properly joined together but they never tell you anything. You stare and wait and they stare back, waiting, in silence. "This is not good," you whisper to yourself, and your reflection agrees. This is what the Book calls a 'negative thought spiral'. You need to get out. Go for a walk. Besides, that's three job application forms you've filled out. You've reworked your C.V. and washed the dishes. That's plenty. That's more than some people do who actually have jobs. You should be out, enjoying your time off, while you still can, because very soon things are going to change. Like the Book says, 'Those who project success, attract success.' You pull your shoulders back and grin at the bathroom mirror forcing yourself to look successful. "Things are going to change," you say out loud. "They are going to change. And when they do, you'll be busy, so busy, you'll wish you had all day to flop around on the sofa."

Reaching for the old cagoule, you hesitate. Instead, you put on the black jacket, the one you wear to interviews, the one that makes you feel slimmer, and start up the street. Outside, frost clings to the shade. Walking quick, with fists clenched in your trouser pockets, your breath steams out ahead of you. The day smells of trampled autumn leaves. The sky is flat, blank. A plastic bag crackles along with the breeze. You have no idea where you're going, but you feel drawn towards the corner shop, towards chocolate biscuits and flicking through garish magazines. Jogging across the street to avoid a bus, you almost run right into her.

"Help me," she says. "It's burning, so it is."

You've seen this old woman before, drifting around the

neighbourhood in her dressing gown. Last week you watched her having an involved, accusation driven argument with the post box. Today, she's addressing the entire street.

"Help. It's burning. It's all burning! Help me."

You lower your head to avoid eye contact and keep walking. She hobbles along the pavement and stops right in front of you. "Now *you're* walking away. Oh! I need help, son!"

There's no way round her. You're close enough to catch the scent of old sweat from her clothes. The wrinkles on her face crumple back revealing watery eyes sensitive to daylight. Hairy lips hunch around her gums, and inside, the mouth is a room without furniture. The mouth speaks.

"I'm frightened, son. It's burning! What can we do? I'm just a wee lassie. I'm on ma own."

You know you should keep walking. Yet, because you're weak willed, you speak, "What's burning?"

"It's all burning. What can we do? And she's got two weans upstairs." The old woman points a curved yellow fingernail towards the flats in front of you.

The air above the building is clear and free of smoke.

"Come. See," she says, turning towards the building. On the back of her head, under a wisp of spider-web hair, you notice two swollen cysts on her scalp: loose lumps the size of testicles. She opens the door to the close and shuffles in, muttering to people only she can see. You follow her into the damp corridor. You warn yourself not to, but you can't help it.

"Do you smell it, son? What can we do? It's burning!"

The stairway smells of wet cardboard, possibly smoke. If there are children upstairs you need to help. You bound up the stairs three at a time. On the first landing you're faced with two doors. One deep breath through your nose reveals... nothing. You knock on the first door. No answer. The door is cool. The other door tells the same story. You race up to the second floor and knock on both doors. "Hello," you call through each letterbox, but no one's home. Are you sure that's smoke you can smell? Cigarette stubs litter the corner of the landing. Probably just kids, sneaking up the stairs for a quick fag.

Back downstairs you notice the old woman opening her front door. "What can we do?" she keeps saying. You decide to check her flat too. Maybe she burned her lunch or something. The air inside her flat has a stale warmth with a lingering odour of kitty litter, but no burning.

The kitchen is clear. The stove is off.

She hobbles through and switches on the TV. Her living room is furnished with a reclining chair facing the television, two electric heaters – one new and one broken – and an unmade bed. She must sleep through here where it's warm. The carpet is patterned with great orange and black swirls. Romance novels lie piled on the floor next to her bed. On her pillow is a novel titled: *The Flame of Desire*. The cover shows a fireman carrying a swooning woman with a torn blouse out of a burning mansion.

You stand next to the bed and watch her yelling at a talk show host and his guest. "You useless buggers! You should be helping me!" She slaps the side of the television, hard.

"Were you making toast?" you ask, but she doesn't hear you.

"I'm all alone and no one's helping me." She turns to you. "I'm frightened. William is away, away to work. There's nobody but me and I'm just a young lassie."

"Who is William?" you ask.

"He's away at work!" she says, shaking her head. "He's never coming back, you know. Never, never, never! William's away. Far away at work."

You pat the armchair. "You're ok, why don't you sit down."

"But what will I do when the fires come? I can't do anything." To demonstrate her point she spreads her arms and gazes down at her knees. For a second the two of you stand, staring at her short, frail body. "Thank God above you came, son. I'll make tea," she says, moving towards the kitchen. "Ma William used to love tea, so he did."

You rub your forehead knowing she'll keep you here for hours if she can. "No tea for me thanks, I have to go." You speak to her loud and slow, the same way you give tourists directions.

She turns, blinks, and starts crying.

"No, no, no. Please don't cry. It's ok. You're ok," you say patting her shoulder. "I'll have some tea. Just a quick cup."

She wipes the tears with the back of her wrist and glares, not trusting that you'll stay. She turns and goes to the kitchen.

You sit on the corner of her bed, staring at the TV while it talks to itself. How are you going to get out of here? You can't spend all day watching telly. What if an employer calls and you're not home? Do you honestly think they'll call back? You see, this, this *right here*, is your problem.

The woman appears in the hall with a mug of tea in each hand and you sit straighter hoping she didn't catch you mumbling to yourself.

"Here ye are, son," she says, handing you the tea and from the pocket of her dressing gown she produces a Kit-Kat.

"Thank you. You're very kind."

Together, you watch Countdown. You sitting with your jacket on and her shouting, "You're useless!" at the contestants. The tea is warm and sweet. You don't usually take sugar but the more you drink the more you get used to it. A commercial break comes on. You put down the empty mug and shove your hands into your jacket pockets. They contain house keys, a tube pass and a postcard leaflet. Someone must have handed the leaflet to you in the street. On the back it reads:

**2-4-1 Drinks.**
**Tuesday nights.**
**At the Space Station.**

On the front is a black and white picture of some dapper chap with a smug smirk. He has hair like a game show host and he's dressed as an astronaut. It crosses your mind that this photo might originally have been part of a 1950's cigarette commercial.

You watch the old woman while she stares open mouthed at a toothpaste advert and wonder how long she has lived here, alone like this? On the windowsill beside her bed is a collection of framed photos. One shows a couple standing rigid outside the front of a house. Another is of a man in uniform. There's a family in winter coats on the beach. You imagine her gazing at these faces every night while she waits for sleep to finally come. You pick up one of the frames and it comes apart in your hands, the back pops off and the glass slides onto your lap. Typical.

"I have to go now," you say, getting to your feet.

"Are you leaving as well?" she says. "Suppose you're away to work?"

"Uh, not exactly."

"So you will be staying for your dinner, then?"

"No, I have to... I have to go to work. I'm sorry."

Her tears start, immediately. "You're away and you're never coming back."

You watch her crying into her hands. Blue light from the TV flickers across her skin. The picture frame lies broken on her bed.

The Book says, 'Every setback is merely an *opportunity*.' You grab the pieces of the picture frame, slip the leaflet of the astronaut under the glass and secure the back by bending the metal clips with your fingernail.

"Look, I've got you a present!" you say, showing her the framed leaflet. "This is a picture of me, at work. I'll leave it here on top of the telly. See? There you are. Now you won't need to feel frightened because I'll always be right here in the room with you."

She wipes tears from her eyes and peers intensely at the photograph.

"That's no you. Can you not tell by looking?"

You pick up the photo and take another look. The astronaut's teeth are Hollywood perfect. His confidence is bullet proof.

"I'm no daft, son. I *know* who that is," she says, giving you a dead bolt stare. "That's your uncle Dennis fae the War."

You look at her and again at the photo.

"Sorry Gran, you're absolutely right," you say, "that is uncle Dennis. But... but you've always said I look just like him, haven't you." You hold the frame next to your face and try to smile like the guy in the picture. Her eyes flit between the astronaut and your most successful grin.

"Aye, I've always said that," she says. "You're just like your uncle Dennis. He was always a good man. So *good*."

"Aye, he was," you say, sensing victory. "And what's more, you were always his favourite, did you know that?"

Her stare softens, wanting to believe.

"Oh definitely. Uncle Dennis would say it all the time. 'She's my number one favourite' he would say."

"My number one favourite," the old woman repeats softly to herself.

You hand her the frame and she leans back into her easy chair, gazing down into the astronaut's smiling eyes. She strokes the outline of the photograph with her finger. Applause from a studio audience bleeds from the TV while you stand for a minute staring down at the cysts growing out of her scalp. Without disturbing her mood, you change the channel on the television to an old black and white musical. She looks up and sways gently along to the music, humming to herself. As quietly as possible, you sneak back along the hall, open the front door and pull it closed behind you.

## Colin's Nation

## Anneliese Mackintosh

---

Enough to feed an army, Mum says. An army.
But what do armies eat?

> Dust.
> Mud.
> Firecrackers.
> Bullets.
> BANGBANGBANG on your plate!

That's what armies eat. Not fairy cakes and salad sandwiches.

But I won't tell Mum she's got it wrong. She's huffing and puffing, which means she's stressed. Stressed is something grown-ups get, and when they get it, it's best not to tell them when they make mistakes.

'Don't worry,' I tell her, 'we haven't got an army coming. Just Samir and his mummy.'

'Lizzie, do be quiet darling,' mutters Mum, 'I'm trying to think.' She huffs and puffs some more. 'Should I have got a Victoria sponge?' She screws up her eyes at the table. 'No. This is enough for High Tea.'

*High Tea.* I see why it's called that: the piles of food are nearly as high as me! Took us aaaaaages to buy all the stuff today. We must have walked over half of Glasgow. We got strawberries and blackberries from the farmer's market and then salmon from the fishmongers on Byres Road (*pooooo-eeeeeeee!*) and then oatcakes from the deli with the boar's head on the wall (YIKES) and then *three* different types of jam from Marks and Sparks (which is actually called Marks and Spencer but grown-ups say Sparks cos it rhymes).

Our flat is *never* normally this full of food.

Mum doesn't take me to the shops much any more. We used to go every weekend, all over the West End, then we'd stop in the Botanics for ice-cream, even when it was raining. I liked that bit best, not because of the ice-cream, even though that was really good, but because of Kibble Palace.

Kibble Palace isn't a real palace because no kings or queens live there. It's actually made of glass and inside it there are trees and statues and fat fish. But it's called a palace so it makes me feel like a princess.

'Bow down to me, Mr. Fish.'
'Here's a coin for you and your fat children.'
'In return you can grant me a wish.'

Sometimes I'm not a princess. I'm a jungle explorer. SWOOSH SWOOSH SWOOSH! as I cut back the leaves.

CRACK! as I whip the elephant to carry me faster.

WHAM! as I shoot a tiger in the eye. And HAHAHA! at the statue of the man who has a monkey as a friend. Silly man.

We didn't go to Kibble Palace today. We polished the china instead.

'Sit down, Lizzie. You're making me nervous.' Mum clasps and unclasps her hands then sits at the head of the table. I sit next to her.

The scone pile comes up to my nose. Can smell the dough. Mmmmmmm.

BZZZZZZZZ.

It's the buzzer!

Mum scrapes back her chair and goes into the hall. 'Hello?' A pause. 'Mrs. Ahmed! Come on up.'

The door screeches open.

'Hello, Mrs. Gordon.' That's Mrs. Ahmed's voice. There's a loud shuffle on the mat. And then a second, quieter shuffle.

The door clicks shut.

I turn around and act surprised. 'Oh, hi.' I smile, but remember that my front tooth fell out last week and I'm gappy.

'Hi, Lizzie,' Samir says quietly. He's wearing new clothes: a bright red t-shirt and jeans. Looks like he's in a washing powder advert.

Mum calls this old pinny I've got on my *Victorian outfit*. I wish I looked like I was in a washing powder advert instead.

Samir sits opposite me and looks at his lap.

'Please, sit down,' Mum chirps, pulling out a chair, which nearly lands on Mrs. Ahmed's foot. Then she goes back to the head of the table.

Our faces peep above the piles of food like cherries on cakes.

'How lovely!' sings Mum, fiddling with a doily. Her voice sounds even more English than usual and about a trillion times posher. 'I've been meaning to do this for *such* a long time, Mrs. Ahmed. It's so *nice* to finally repay the favour.'

I've been to Mrs. Ahmed's house twice. The first time it was raining so Samir showed me his toy cars and we played Etch-a-Sketch. The second time was in the summer and we went into the back yard and I found a four-leaf clover and Samir told me I was clever.

Both times Mrs. Ahmed cooked, but it was nothing like the stuff here. Mrs. Ahmed made a lot of pink food.

PINK cakes.
PINK pasties.
PINK crackers.

It all tasted sickly and spicy and strange. But the second time we went I liked it more. I think I'll be used to it next time we go, and I'll probably really REALLY like it by about the fifth or six time.

'Tea's brewed!' Mum pours out four cups. She doesn't normally use the china teapot. Usually she dips the bags in the cups and throws them in the bin. 'I got this tea from the deli.' She passes a cup and saucer over to Mrs. Ahmed, and then one to Samir. 'It's Assam.'

Mrs. Ahmed coughs.

'Do help yourself,' Mum says, picking up a fairy cake with a fluttery laugh.

I want a slab of gingerbread and a scone. I reach out both hands.

'Thank you, Mrs. Gordon,' smiles Mrs. Ahmed, 'but Samir and I won't be eating today.'

'You won't?' Mum's mouth is full of fairy wings.

'There are some pink wafer biscuits over here, Mrs. Ahmed?' I suggest.

'It's Ramadan,' says Mrs. Ahmed.

Mum swallows with a gulp. 'Oh no. Oh, I'm so sorry.' She drops the rest of the cake and starts wiping her face with a doily.

'What's *ram it down*?' I ask.

Samir's still looking into his lap.

'Ramadan,' Mrs. Ahmed tells me, 'is a time when many Muslims do not to eat or drink while it's light outside.'

'Like owls?' I ask. 'They eat at night. Except in that story, the one about the owl who was afraid of the dark.'

Mrs. Ahmed laughs. 'No, Lizzie, it's not exactly like that.'

'I'm so sorry,' Mum sighs. She's finally stopped rubbing her face with the doily. 'I didn't think.'

I look outside. 'It's nearly dark now.'

We all breathe in the sticky air. The smells are swirling. The salmon, wherever it is, is mixing with the gingerbread, and the ham is mixing with the Bakewell tarts.

'Can I still have my scone please, Mummy?' I ask quietly. 'I'm not an owl.'

'No you can't,' she snaps.

'What?' My eyes sting. I look at Samir but he's staring at the wall behind me.

Mum huffs and puffs for a bit, but then stops and smiles. 'Why don't you go to your room, Lizzie? With Samir?

Mrs. Ahmed and I will have a chat in the living room, away from all this... all this...' she snorts: 'nonsense.'

I jump down from my chair and run to the door. 'Come on, Sammy.'

'*Samir*,' Mum says, which is funny, because she never normally minds me calling him that.

Samir's still staring at the wall like he's in a trance. The photo of Great Gramps Gordon stares back, in a trance too. Great Gramps Gordon has what Mum calls a *stiff upper lip*. I wonder if that's what makes his moustache prick up at both corners.

'Go on, Samir,' says Mrs. Ahmed.

Samir slides off his seat and follows me.

I sit on the bed. He sits on the bed.

There's a cat outside, on the fence of the tenement opposite. I can't tell if that's Sukie or Ruffles. One's a tabby and the other's a tortie, but they both look the same in this light, lovely wee things.

Samir swings his legs. His heels bang into the craft chest under my bed.

THUD THUD THUD THUD

'When does Rammy-dan stop?' I ask.

He shrugs.

'Want to play a game?'

He shakes his head.

THUD THUD THUD THUD THUD THUD

'I made it,' I say.

'Made what?'

'A game. It's a cross between Snakes and Ladders and Monopoly.'

His eyes go bigger.

'You have to get really rich and build lots of houses, and if you get a ladder it helps you build faster, but if a snake comes into your house it eats you.'

He looks out of the window and shrugs again.

Samir is being quiet, like when I first met him. We were five then. He didn't speak much English so Mum taught him words like *difficult* and *brilliant* in the car. We've been driving Samir for four years. In the morning we take him to school then after that he comes back to ours until Mrs. Ahmed finishes work.

Mr. and Mrs. Ahmed are nice. They let us have free curries from Mr. Ahmed's Tandoori Restaurant. We eat a lot of curry now. Most days, actually. Mainly carry-outs. Sometimes meals out. Mum even puts cold curry in my lunchbox. She says free food is not to be sniffed at, but I can't help sniffing when I eat curry, it just happens.

I look around my room for Things To Do. If I was on my own I'd play with my Tiny Tears. I've got a whole shelf of them. REALLY pretty dolls with REALLY blonde hair and REALLY pale skin and holes where they REALLY WET THEMSELVES (only with water, but I tried it with orange squash once and it looked proper!) But Tiny Tears are just for girls, so I need to think of something else.

Fuzzy Felt? Bit fiddly.
Lego? Yawnnnnnnnnnnnnnn.
Baked-bean jigsaw? Ick. Too hard.

'What about dressing up?' I ask, bouncing off the bed. 'I'll be a vampire.'

'You're always a vampire.'

'Okay then. If you don't want to do dressing up, what *do* you want to do?'

He groans. Maybe he's dying of hunger.

I sit on the carpet and cross my legs like in assembly. 'Come and join me,' I say, doing a funny English voice, 'for some tea.'

'I can't drink -' he starts, but then sees me pinching the air, pretending to hold a teapot.

'You're allowed this type of tea, aren't you?'

'Okay.' He plops onto the floor. His t-shirt slides up:

his tummy's got black hair on it. My toes go tingly.

I pinch my fingers on the other hand to make a cup and then pour us both a tea. 'There you go, Sammy. Oh no. You're not holding it right. Pinch your thumb and forefinger together like this. Then stick up your little finger. That's better. You could drink tea with the Queen like that. Okay. Now lift it to your lips and drink. Little sips.'

Samir lifts up his cup but doesn't drink. 'Are your hands bleeding?' he asks suddenly.

'What?' I stop pinching my fingers and look at my hand. 'Where?'

'My dad says your hands are bleeding.'

'What? No. There's no blood.'

'He says your family's hands have blood on them.'

'That's a silly thing to say, Sammy. Of course they haven't. Look.'

He throws his cup on the floor. 'My dad doesn't lie.'

'Are you hungry? Is it making you feel funny? Drink some tea. You'll feel better.' I do a big sluuuuUUURRP!

He shakes his head. 'That picture.'

'What picture?'

'That picture in your kitchen. The old man with the moustache.'

'Oh! The photo of Great Gramps. You like it? That's a VERY old photograph. It's *two centuries* old. That's two hundred years, Sammy. Great Gramps looks like a very important man, doesn't he?' I grin. 'Hey, I know! Let's dress up like him! We'll need a cardboard box for a cart, maybe a toothbrush for the moustache...'

'No! No!' Samir wriggles around like his insides hurt. 'Do you know what your granddad -'

'My *great* granddad.'

'- what your *great* granddad is sitting on?'

'Aye, course I do,' I say proudly. 'It's the Indian Railway.'

'And who are those other men in the photo?'

'The shadowy men? I don't know. Come on, Sammy, do the tea party properly. Now would you pass me the sugar please?'

Samir passes me some sugar but he pours it over my cup for a lot longer than you would with real sugar. Tastes disgusting if you put too much in, but I drink anyway. I wonder if he can read my mind. If he can he'll know I wrote his name on a heart-shaped sticker and stuck it in my diary last night.

'My dad,' Samir says in a strange, low voice, 'says you're taking something.'

'Taking what? What am I taking?'

'I'm not saying.' He shakes his head.

'Say it.'

'It's a bad word.'

'I won't tell.'

Samir wrinkles his nose and whispers: 'piss.'

'Taking *piss*?'

'Sssh! Yes. He says you go to our restaurant all the time. And he says that a few lifts are worth much less than a thousand chicken tikka masalas. And he says that from now on...'

'From now on what?'

'You can forget your extra green chillies.' He thuds his feet against the carpet, a softer thud this time.

thhhhhhh thhhhhhh thhhhhhh thhhhhhh

'Samir, I don't understand.'

'I think,' he says, twisting and untwisting his lips, making them all sore, 'that maybe we're running out of food.'

'Is that why you're so hungry? Is that why you're doing Rammy-dan?'

'My dad says that all he ever brought to Scotland were his special pakoras, but your great granddad didn't take any pakoras to India. He took-'

'What did he take?'

Samir swallows hard. 'Piss.'

'No, Samir. No he didn't. He probably took stuff like wood and metal to make the railway. Now don't be mean or

I'll tell your mum. Please drink your tea.'

'Don't want to.' Samir crosses his arms and shuffles back on the floor. 'It wasn't just your great granddad anyway. He went with lots of other men and they took lots of piss. I think the boss was called Colin, because my dad called it Colin's nation. And lots of people died.'

'But Great Gramps was Scottish,' I say quickly. 'He said *aye* like me and drank whiskey like my dad. Scottish people aren't bad, Sammy.' I try to laugh. 'Dad says that *English* men did nasty things once... My mummy's not nasty though. She's nice.'

Samir frowns. 'Well my dad told me,' he blurts, 'about when he lived in Kolkata, and about what Colin's nation did to the tea.'

'Tea?' I remember my cup and pinch the handle, but the look on Samir's face makes me let go.

'I wonder if my mum is ready to take me home yet,' he murmurs.

'You can't go!'

'Why not?'

'Because you haven't finished your-' I stop talking and look at his eyes. They're not like Samir's eyes anymore. They're like the eyes on the fat fish in Kibble Palace: watery, cloudy. 'Never mind.'

I pick a scab on my arm from where I fell yesterday at playtime. It comes off. Blood drips on my hand.

Samir gasps. 'Blood.'

I wipe it on my pinny. 'Gone.' But it comes back and starts to drip again. I put my mouth on the cut and suck.

'We can't be friends any more,' Samir tells me.

'Why?'

'I'm old enough to get the bus now. And I'm joining the after school club.'

There's wet around my lips. I don't know if it's spit or blood.

Rain patters hard at the window. I wonder what Sukie and Ruffles are doing to keep warm.

Screeeeeeeeeeeeech.

That's the front door.

BOOOOOOOOOOOOOOOOOOOM!!!!!!!!!!!!!!!!!!!!!!!!!!!!!!

That's a boot on the doormat.
I wait.
'Halloooo gang! I'm home early!' yells Dad. 'And I've brought carry-out!'
I picture the bag of meat in his hand. My tongue aches.
Is my daddy part of Colin's nation?
It's pitch black outside. Samir's probably allowed to eat something now. I look at him, then wipe my arm and walk out, past the living room, where Mum and Mrs. Ahmed are talking. Mum's still huffing and puffing.
Dad is standing at the door, looking down at me. His moustache pricks up at both corners.
'Daddy!' I shout.
I run over and cling onto his leg, *tight tight tight*. I'm not going to let him go. Not ever. We're going to stay here, on the mat, in the doorway. I breathe in his smell: dust, mud, firecrackers, and green chillies.

## Means of ID

## Tawona Sitholé

He stared out blankly at the scene below, seventeen floors away. This was not the Great Britain he had imagined. He realised he was still holding his mobile phone. He tucked it into his jeans and got ready to leave.

Locking and double-checking his door, he left the flat without any thought of having something to eat. He had no appetite, and even if he did, there was no food in the house. A trip to the shops was overdue. The lift had just been cleaned, but even the strong detergent could not totally over-power the usual stuffy smell. The graffiti in green marker pen glared at him from the pimpled metal skin. He had a moment to himself before being interrupted on the third floor, as four teens came bustling in. The lone girl of the group had one of those fancy mobile phones with extra-loud music player and it was blasting out some rap song. Jaya stood perfectly still and absently stared straight ahead, pre-tending not to notice the attention-grabbing antics of the teens, as they sang along. When the doors eventually opened on the ground floor, the young teens excitedly ran out of the lift, shouting an array of urban slogans. One of the chants Jaya managed to pick up was an enthusiastic *'what's up my nigga?'*. He cursed the mainstream success of hip-hop. He zigzagged round the puddles, as he hastily made his way through the courtyard and along towards the bus stop.

A plane flew noisily overhead, reminding him of his own big bird that took off in the sun and landed him in the snow. In one swoop the transformation was done. No more picking fruits off a tree - here, the tree had a big sign saying *buy one get one free*; a chicken was no longer a feathered creature that had to be hunted round the yard, but instead submitted to the hunter, already plucked and cleaned. He chuckled to himself thinking how quickly he was becoming like that chicken. Eating tinned food and ready-made meals. Taking the bus to places within walking distance, he had submitted to convenience. As he was learning, change was mostly subtle. He quietly worried about the implications.

'You got the time there pal?'

It was another bunch of kids, younger this time, who ran off laughing before he could even respond. They seemed to just enjoy the idea of having some dialogue with him. He arrived at the mutilated bus shelter, closely followed by three guys who looked in their late teens. They were mid-flow in a verbal re-enactment of some epic brawl they were supposed to have been in. One of the young guys kept spitting on the pavement. Jaya looked away, choosing to suffer the audio-only version. By the time the bus turned up, it had started drizzling.

The bus driver called Jaya back to the little window and took an extra long moment scrutinising his bus pass before waving him on, almost reluctantly. Jaya couldn't help feeling annoyed; if he was a super criminal, master forger, you think he'd forge something more substantial than a bus pass. Jaya had a little system for picking a seat on the bus. His preferred spot was anywhere in the middle; far enough from the front to avoid having to move too much, and not too near the back where he felt vulnerable. After a quick inspection, the only spot available turned out to be one seat away from the very back of the bus. Not one for the upper deck, he made his way to the back of the bus. He looked up to see the would-be brawlers, from his bus stop, helping an elderly lady with her grocery bags and then into her seat. It didn't change his feelings about spitting.

Without warning, a voice fired from behind him,

'Where you fae big man?'

Recoiling from the shot, Jaya answered pleasantly but minimally - aware that the attention of the whole bus was probably now on him. The track-suited stranger's distinct Glaswegian dialect threw Jaya back to the time when he'd first arrived here. He remembered how the accent had stunned him early on; not quite the BBC newsreaders' enunciation that he expected. In the meantime, the questions were coming steadily. The guy wanted to know Jaya's name; where he was from; why he was here; how long he was staying and what had made him leave his home. Jaya felt obliged to affirm how poor it was where he was from, and how grateful he was to be finally away from all that trouble.

He couldn't avoid the questions wherever he went: *what is it like?; what do you eat over there?; do you miss home?; where do you prefer?*

But at least people were interested in him. Sometimes it felt like people were trying to work him out for themselves. The news suggested he was a label or a thing - asylum seeker, refugee or migrant worker; pop culture depicted him as a rapper or singer; to the young couple next door he was a neighbour; to the elderly people he often found himself chatting to at bus stops and other unlikely places, he was 'son'. There was something homely about a place where elders called you son and others called you mate or pal.

'Take care big man, that's my stop after the lights.'

The chatterbox announced his departure, leaving Jaya thinking about how in Zimbabwe, traffic lights were known as 'robots'. It was one of those expressions that had become redundant since he moved here, along with his own native tongue, which only got aired when he was on the phone to his wife and two young daughters, or else his parents.

A couple of school kids got on the bus, and he couldn't help an instinctive questioning of why they were not in school. He thought back to his own school days, tough times but also fun times. The school experience was not complete without nicknames. The more you resisted, the more they stuck. He thought again about all the tags that came with being a foreigner - an African. It made him laugh at himself for being so affected now that it was happening to him when, back in his own school days, he called immigrants names. It would mostly be some derivative of their home country, or something to do with being a wanderer; it seemed like nothing at the time. Just then there was a loud crashing noise.

The bus immediately pulled over to the side of the road amidst the murmurs and general disturbance mixed with slight panic. The driver headed up onto the top deck of the bus cursing under his breath. The driver ordered everyone off the bus, while he communicated on his walkie-talkie.

Stepping outside, Jaya joined the other passengers in surveying the damaged window. The glass was totally shattered; it was lucky that no one had been injured. Across the street was another billboard; this one was about 'Homecoming Scotland'. All being well, he would be having his own homecoming at the end of the year; a chance to catch up with his family again. The two women behind him were locked in a loud conversation about some wonderful new diet. In this place of plenty, people chose to eat very little; in a place so cold even the buildings wear jackets, many people chose to wear as little as possible. And the fuss people here made over the slightest bit of sunshine! He remembered how he used to make fun of the locals, but in a place where a summer's day is not necessarily a sunny day, now he was just as overexcited to see the sun as they were. He pulled the hood of his jacket over his head and stood waiting patiently for the replacement bus.

His bank was a few doors along from the big bar/restaurant; an old church conversion. It was such a contrast to his native land where conversion was denominated by the new churches sprouting everywhere. It was a serious competition to see who was dressed best in Sunday best. From the fathers in suits, to the proud women in their uniforms dragging their children along, all flocking to hear the flamboyant, sly preachers - the natives were fervently carrying on from where the old missionaries had left off. There was no turning in graves for those old ghosts. Those were the colonies, but the religion of money was one without non-believers; and right now Jaya was off to worship. After trying his bankcard in the wall, he reluctantly headed inside. With houses of worship on every street, the power of this force was everywhere. Even in Glasgow, the sectarian divide had nothing on this supreme religion that towered over all. Across the ocean in America at least they were more open about their love, declaring on every note how 'in god they trust'.

'C-AN Y-OU F-ILL THIS OU-T A-ND BRI-NG IT BA-CK HE-RE', the lady behind the glass screen shouted, finishing off with a forced professional smile. Other customers gave Jaya curious looks. The woman had totally mispronounced his name, but now was not the time to protest his proficiency in English as a second language. An elderly lady offered to help him but he politely insisted he was fine. After filling in the form he had to produce some ID, and then it was done. Now he just had to wait to see if the bank would approve his overdraft application. He came out of the bank feeling exhausted. Maybe it was all the strain; maybe it was the fact he hadn't eaten. It was another one of those moments when it felt like life in the first world, of a second-class citizen, from the third world.

As he boarded his return bus home, he noticed an older friendly lady from his building. He thought he'd follow the example of the brawlers from earlier on and help her with her bags. As they slowly walked towards the tall grey towers, she was relaying to him her events of the day. Touching the heart-shaped badge on her smart jacket she explained that she had been to see her husband. For the first time, Jaya realised it was Valentine's Day.

Her Jim now lived in an elderly care home, as she put it, 'he wasn't coping very well with simple things'. Jaya wondered what that said of life here. Back home the family were automatic carers; it wasn't even a question. The old lady told him that she visited every week; so that's where she had been going all those times he'd seen her at the bus stop. She was explaining that, due to the dementia, every time she visited her husband, he asked who she was. She fumbled through her handbag and pulled out a photo. They both stopped as she showed Jaya what looked like a holiday photo of a middle-aged couple. It's a sunny day and they are standing at the edge of the sea, water up to the knees; both with trousers rolled up and holding ice cream cones. She explained that she now had to go through the usual routine of pulling out that old picture of the two of them together, just to get him to remember who she was. Jaya only managed to make some odd comment about the picture, and they continued on in silence. She got off on the fourth floor, smiling warmly at him as he handed her bag over.

'Take care son,' she said before the lift doors separated them.

Finally arriving outside his door, it felt like ages since he had left. Just as he walked into the flat, his mobile phone went off. He jumped, startled by the familiar ring tone. He closed his eyes briefly, as he took in breath, then he looked at the caller ID.

## The Donaldson Boy

### Aidan Moffat

---

Dear Police,

This is a confession, although it is an anonymous one, so you may be inclined to consider it a boast. I can assure you that this is not my intention. As a woman of retirement age who has spent almost every available Sunday in one Church or another, I can solemnly swear that I feel a genuine sense of remorse for my crime. Although, admittedly, these feelings are not so strong as to compel me to provide you with my name, and I should hope that you have more important matters to attend to anyway. Mine was a petty crime, and thanks to your recent cost-cutting exercises in the area and a reduction in the number of local officers, I expect you would have neither the time nor the resources to concern yourself with the mere theft of a mobile telephone.

But before I confess, allow me to paint a background that may encourage you to sympathise with my very minor offence. I have lived in the village of West Kilbride all my life and have always loved it here. I am active in the community, I am well known and, if I may say so myself, a respected denizen of our little hamlet. I was lucky enough to be able to retire before my sixtieth birthday, but unfortunately this was due to my husband's early and sudden death by heart attack. His life insurance policy paid quite handsomely, so once it was cashed I had no further need to work and chose to remain in our home by myself. I continue to socialise and have many friends from the surrounding towns of the region who often come to visit and stay, but for the most part I live in our three-bedroom cottage alone (pets not included). This was never a cause for concern until recently. Ever since North Ayrshire Council decided to close the local police station on Alton Street and swiftly reduce our community officers in number until we were left with only two, it seems that the village has become overrun with vandalism, hooliganism, littering, foul language and the deadly menace of so-called "boy racing". My neighbours and I have all fallen victim to the defacement of our homes with hideous and indecipherable graffiti; we have suffered the drunken destruction of our private property, including rainwater down-pipes, garden fences and motor vehicles – there was even an incident involving a broken living-room window. There is the constant roar of revelry between the hours of 7 pm and 2 am, including extreme profanity, obnoxious singing and violent battle cries; there is the ever-present detritus of said revelry, e.g. lager cans, beer and wine bottles (often smashed to pieces), food packaging etc.; and, of course, the aforementioned "boy racing", making our intimate little streets extremely dangerous and potentially lethal, not to mention the noise pollution caused by the constant thump and hiss of the inhumanly fast music that the drivers of these vehicles seem to use as inspiration.

There is one individual who is guilty of all of the above and much, much more, a particularly nasty young ruffian – a "Ned" as us Scots call such characters – by the name of Steven Donaldson, or "Donny" as he is known to his legion of thugs. I should expect that you are already familiar with both him and his family. His mother and father are similarly dislikeable, as were his grandparents, and I know for a fact that they have all been arrested for various offences over the years, including at least one incidence of very serious theft. They remain very unpopular in the village, and I have often found myself crossing to the other side of the street whenever their hideously obese figures come into view. Yes, fatness seems to be the family curse and young Steven is by far the biggest of them all, his shaven head doing his repugnant, chubby mug no favours whatsoever. He is physically quite monstrous, but his massive bulk seems to afford him a threatening presence and the local "Neds" appear to revere both him and his vehicle. He drives a ridiculous little red

Vauxhall Corsa adorned with those laughable sports stripes that yobs seem to favour – two parallel white lines painted from the front tip of the bonnet to the back edge of the roof. How he manages to squeeze his hideously flabby body into the driver's seat of such a small car is a mystery to all but the greatest of physicists, but nevertheless he can be seen at the wheel almost every night, racing through the village at dangerous and illegal speeds whilst more than likely over the acceptable alcohol limit. He and his foul companions tend to congregate in the train station car park even though it is clearly stated in the sign posted there that such loitering is strictly prohibited and punishable by law. I live very close to the station (forgive me for not revealing precisely where) and his constant presence has me living in a state of perpetual terror.

One Thursday, a few weeks ago, as I was catching the train to Glasgow to spend the day shopping for a new dress to wear to a friend's granddaughter's wedding, I saw the Donaldson boy's car parked at the station. It was empty, however, and he was nowhere to be seen, having left the vehicle on display at a jaunty angle across two spaces so as to attract attention. The reason for this became apparent as I approached: there was an A4 sheet of paper sellotaped to the inside of the window, advertising that the car was for sale, including a mobile telephone number for potential purchasers. I paid this no mind at the time although I was highly irritated by the way the vehicle deliberately used two spaces, flaunting a complete disregard and contempt for the car park's rules. I went to Glasgow as planned, found a suitable dress and a pair of shoes to match, met with a friend for an early evening dinner, then caught the 7.45 train back home. When the train made its regular stop at Stevenston en route, a young girl, who was outrageously drunk and could barely stand, sat down on the opposite seat from my own. She was quite clearly what might be described as a "Nedette" – a young, female yob dressed in standard issue tracksuit and decorated with grotesque jewellery. She also smelled quite vile, of cigarettes and cheap tonic wine, but thankfully

this was her only intrusion into my otherwise peaceful journey because moments after she sat down and sent a text
message on her mobile telephone, she fell asleep (or perhaps
passed out is a more appropriate way to describe it). She had
left her phone lying on the seat beside her and I noticed that
it was exactly the same make and model as my own – and
this is when I was inspired to commit my crime. When the
train pulled into West Kilbride she was sound asleep, and I
waited until the rest of the passengers in my carriage had
disembarked before I very quickly and discreetly snatched
her telephone and stashed it in the bag that held my new
dress. I must confess that it was all very thrilling. When I
walked through the car park, the Donaldson boy's car was
there (but in a different two spaces) with the sign still in the
window, so I nonchalantly read and memorised the number,
repeating it constantly in my mind until I reached my
kitchen and found something to scribble it down on. I was
breathing very heavily by this time, still dizzy from the rush
of the theft, my plan beginning to overwhelm me, and I found
that I had to sit down for a few moments to compose myself.

Not for too long, though – I knew that I had to act
quickly as the young "Nedette" could easily arrange to have
her phone disconnected once she arrived home. So I removed
it from my bag and, employing the modern technique of "text
speak" that I have absorbed from such types of correspondence with my English niece, sent my first anonymous text
message to Steven Donaldson, in which I am ashamed to say
I used the same kind of coarse language and patois that I
constantly hear from "Donny" and his like. It read thus:

## UR CAR IS PISH YA BALDY BASTARD :-(

There was no reply for a good ten minutes, but just as
I was beginning to feel disappointed, the telephone beeped.
The reply was utterly predictable. It simply read:

## WHO R U (There was no question mark.)

Obviously I had no intention of revealing my identity, so I replied with this:

## U NEED A BIGGER MOTOR YA FAT CUNT

This seemed to anger him a little more than the previous message but did not improve his imagination or punctuation. The reply was simply:

## WHO THE FUK IS THIS

The messages were generating exactly the response I had hoped for, and by now I was positively exhilarated. My third was:

## HAV U EVR SEEN UR COCK, FATTY? LOL

You'll notice that I used the acronym "LOL" for this one. I meant this in the "Laugh Out Loud" or "Lots Of Laughter" sense but instantly regretted it because the Donaldson boy could have mistaken it for "Lots Of Love" and presumed the message was from a playful friend. To rectify this, I quickly sent another message that made my feelings clear:

## I FUKN H8 U YA PORKY POOF

It was at this point he attempted to call. Of course, I didn't answer, leaving the phone to ring out. Minutes later, the phone rang again, and this time it was the automated answer phone service to inform me that he had left a message. On listening, I found said message to be incredibly aggressive, horribly violent and full of profanity, making the intention to find and kill me extremely clear. I was initially quite shaken by it but also felt vindicated – his behaviour was exactly as I had expected and precisely the kind of which the village is now awash with and which must be eradicated. I composed myself once again and sent him a new text message, this time threatening him with the same sort of violence he intended to use on me:

## AM GAUNY CHIB U YA CUNT

This prompted another call, which again I ignored. There was no message this time, although he did make three attempts to get through. When these proved unsuccessful, he sent this message:

## CUM AHED THEN UR FUKN DED

To which I immediately replied:

## UR GETTIN SLASHT A THE WEEKND - WATCH UR BAK YA PUDGY PRICK

Unfortunately, I'm afraid this is where our correspondence had to end, as the telephone ceased to function. I was more than a little disappointed that our dialogue was so brief and had been terminated just as I began to gain confidence. I can only presume that our little "Nedette" had reported the phone lost or stolen and had the number deactivated, so I have no idea if there was ever a reply to my final message. I suspect that there would have been, and hopefully the lack of any kind of response would have frustrated the fat cunt even further. My intention had been to give the Donaldson boy a taste of the fear that he has instilled in me these past few months and I hope that, if only for the littlest while, my plan was successful. While it will certainly have had no lasting effect on the boy, it pleases me greatly to think that for at least the duration of one weekend, "Donny" was constantly looking over his shoulder and suspicious even of his own friends - and I was responsible! It has helped me to cope with his constant, threatening presence, although I still daren't venture outside beyond a certain hour. But now, when I see the Neds in the train station car park, surrounding that ludicrous little car that has yet to be sold, I find myself being able to giggle a little.

So there is my confession. I would have liked to return the stolen phone along with this letter, but the following day was filled with a tremendous panic which found me throwing it into the sea, so I'm afraid it will be halfway to Arran by now.

Yours sincerely,

# The Hostel in Junction Street

## Kapka Kassabova

There are people who believe that your destiny catches up with you. But 'catches up' is the wrong phrase. There are places in the world that *contain* your destiny. It sits there, like a skin waiting for you to walk into it, and assume its shape, and become you.

For me, that place turned out to be right here, in Junction Street. This city contained me all along, since before the day of my birth in Katowice, which some get mixed up with Katyn where lots of Polish officers were slaughtered by the Red Army. No, Katowice doesn't even have a massacre to its name. It's just a dump in the former Eastern bloc. But I digress.

('You are the best digression of my life,' Jackson used to say.)

We arrived in Edinburgh in the summer of 2005, me and Jackson. The streets were full of people with matted hair and painted faces who looked like extras from *Braveheart*. They seemed about to lay siege to the Castle. It turned out to be a G8 protest. They left behind garbage and graffiti, but we had other things to worry about. For example, where we were going to live from now on. Jackson knew this guy, also ex-Army, now a real estate developer. Dan was English and had big chops for a face. He was a bit of a cowboy, but he was the only person we knew between the two of us. He proved quite useful – well, at least that's how we felt at first, because he offered us one of his cheaper flats to stay in, at mates' rates.

(Here in Scotland they say 'stay' instead of 'live', as if you're in a hotel. 'Where do you stay?' people ask, as if living is an overstatement, as if nothing is permanent.)

Make up your mind, Renata *Kowalska,* Dan would
say to me, accentuating my surname like it was a big joke,
are you Polish or are you American, or are you a fucking
double agent? He'd laugh with his mouth open, and his
chops would shake. I laughed too. What the hell, at least he
could pronounce my name. He didn't like ambiguous things,
Dan, and I guess my mixed accent confused him. He fancied
himself as a straight-talking kind of a guy, although his
real estate deals were far from straight. He also tried to grope
my ass once at a party, when he was drunk and Jackson
was looking the other way, but I didn't mind Dan as much as
other people did – Dan had no friends, only serial girlfriends
– and he was quite good to me, in his own way. I last saw
Dan when he came round to the flat to tell me he was
leaving Edinburgh. He was in a hurry, like the police were
following him.

'You can stay in this flat, I don't need it,' he said. 'And
I don't need any rent from you.' He was moving to Spain,
temporarily, I forget the details.

I was trying to tell him about the building, about my
dreams, I even showed him some of the paintings in
progress. I thought I was being reasonable, but he kept looking at me and shaking his head.

'Renata Kowalska,' he said, this time without exagger-
ating my surname, 'You are a good woman, but you're a nut-
ter. Just like Jackson. Suit yourself anyway, and good luck.'

I was surprised to see him upset, and then he
slammed the door.

That night, I had a dream in which Dan was walking,
small and dishevelled, across a burning field. I kept paying
him rent for a few weeks, and then the bank said my payments had been returned. There was no such account under
such a name. It didn't surprise me. My dreams were always
reliable, more than reality anyway. Dreams are like children:
you just have to know how to connect with them.

So we moved into this big, grotty, top-floor flat of Dan's
in Junction Street, Leith. It had half a window's view of the
sea. 'Imagine,' Jackson said, 'between here and Norway,

there's sweet fuck-all.' This made us immensely happy. It was an old-style high-ceilinged flat with an original fire-place and floorboards, but there were burnt spoons on the kitchen floor when we arrived, and rat turds on the mattresses. The bathroom window was broken and pigeons had been inside. We had to throw everything out and fumigate the place.

'Wow, I never thought I'd live inside Trainspotting,' I said to Jackson, and he said, 'Better Trainspotting than Shallow Grave.' Between the two of us – a Polish American and an Aussie – that's all we knew about Edinburgh.

Even though we were both unemployed, we were together at last, after eighteen months of correspondence around the world, me in Krakow, him in Afghanistan and Britain. His army days were over, and I was happy to be out of Poland. My little experiment of living there for a couple of years as a 'real' Pole and a practicing artist hadn't worked out. But had I not done it, I wouldn't have met Jackson.

It happened in my first month in Poland, in the summer. I was doing street portraiture. This guy saunters up to me, angular and sun-burnt and extroverted in a gawky way, with a crew cut and Jesus sandals. He has an army ruck-sack and a guitar.

'Gidday,' he goes. 'I know I've got a big ugly nose, but can you do a portrait of me to send to my mum in Brisbane?'

He was on leave from the British Army. We spent the two weeks together in my top-floor flat in Krakow near the pigeons, and the whole thing made perfect sense, like one of my dreams. For me, it was all happening at once – living back in Poland again after ten years in the US, living the artist's life, and now this. I remember thinking, even then, that he seemed unpredictable at times, especially for a tough army type. Once, when we were on this huge bridge, he hopped up on the stone railing and just walked along there for a while. Everyone stopped to watch in horror. It was like he could be walking next to me one moment, and gone the next. And he seemed to *enjoy* that. When he left we both cried at the airport, and then it was letters and emails for an eternity.

Everyone said I was nuts. I didn't know the guy, we'd literally met in the street, what did I know about his past, and god knows what he was up to in Afghanistan (he didn't talk about that much in his letters, he talked about how he was learning Polish from a mate), and anyway what sort of a joker's name was Jackson - isn't it supposed to be a surname? But I knew. I had dreams in which we were living somewhere in a room near the pigeons, and the city was far below. Or where we were sleeping on mattresses in a big, echoey, dripping hall like a cave.

('Be careful, Renata,' an old artist friend of my parents' said to me at the time. He'd lived through it all and even been to prison in the Communist days. 'Be careful; idealism is the other face of opportunism. They are like the Janus twins.')

Eighteen months later, we'd seen each other twice, and we were still writing. I hadn't met anyone else, and Jackson said he thought of me every single night, even when they were being shelled. He said he was sick of having no home, said he wanted to hit civvy street and start again, from scratch, with me. I didn't miss America, and I didn't want to be in Poland any longer – I didn't belong there anymore. Jackson didn't want to return to Brisbane – red-neck town, he called it – so Edinburgh was perfect. Neutral ground, we thought.

Between the two of us we had some money saved up, so the first few months we walked about the city, climbed up Arthur's Seat, poked around the old town lanes, the usual stuff you do in a new place. We didn't let go of each other. Everything we saw, smelt and felt, we did together. It was our city!

And Leith was our neighbourhood! It smelled of sour sea, wet stone, and booze. And on still days a cosy stench spread over the city – one part men's socks, one part yeast. It was the breweries. People so pale it was a miracle they were still alive propped up the old bars from morning till morning, shuffled around corners littered with cigarette butts, and muttered through the black stubs of their teeth.

Along Leith Walk, Polish shops mushroomed like a fungal infection, their nostalgic wares lining the windows – tins of gherkins, crumbly white bread, smoked sausage, communist-shaped biscuits from my childhood. I sometimes went in just to swap a few words in Polish. Along Junction Street, little delis sold transparent salami and French cheeses, and right next door, Indian and Pakistani shops sold ugly things made from plastic. The men in those shops were unshaven and the women were strangely inert. Lots of people around here looked either like they'd had some sort of accident or were about to.

Here in Leith I found everything I needed: the menstrual red of brick, the tomb-grey of stone, the black of soot, the sepia of the sky, the murk of the river, the graveyard-lush green of the riverbanks in spring. And of course I was with the love of my life, finally, finally. I was in my thirties already, and I'd never had a love of my life before. There were some adjustments at first – like the fact that my paints were soon all over the floor, and I didn't like washing up until all our dishes were piled up at the sink, whereas he was used to order, clothes folded sharp, boots shining at all times. But when it's the love of your life, and you've waited for eighteen months and bet everything on it, you just try. True, he'd sometimes go weird, and quite early on he'd have these moods, either too cheerful, or completely flat, when he'd look at me with blank eyes and say, 'It's this city, it's doing my head in.' I just held him and he shivered like he was ill, but he didn't say more, and neither did I. I preferred to resolve things with sex and a walk by the Water of Leith. In those long months of letters, we'd talked ourselves to death. Sometimes he'd strum his guitar. He only knew how to play one tune on it, a Sting song.

(He said in his letters, and I've kept them all: 'If I get blown to smithereens tomorrow, you'll be all right. Because you're from outer space. I'm the one who'd be lost without you. I've always been a bit lost to be honest. Sometimes it's like *I want* to get blown to smithereens, you know?')

The truth is, I was painting, and he didn't know what

to do. I was constantly thinking up ideas for him, but he wasn't taken with any of them. He didn't want to work for anyone anymore, he said, he wanted to do his own thing – it's just that he didn't know what that was. Apparently that's common for ex-army guys. He still went out every morning at 6am to run and do press-ups along the river, and he was gone for hours. Sometimes he'd go to the top of Arthur's Seat and back. And just when I was starting to worry about him, I noticed the building across the road.

I always sat at the bedroom window under the pigeon-shat cupola, to smoke my first morning cigarette – I'd gone back to smoking in Poland – but it was only now that I took real notice of it. It was hard to miss, really, and yet I'd missed it. Or rather, something in me had rejected it, as if I didn't want to investigate. But now I did. And the more I looked at it, the more I couldn't look away.

It was a bulky, Gothic stone building, darkened by time and soot. Its windows were all boarded up, all except one on the upper floor, which had a single, crucifix-shaped bar. Its little sharp turrets pointed at the sky like hands clasped in prayer. That was in the summer of 2006. By the autumn, Dan had bought or leased the building, even though it was a protected heritage site, and Jackson took charge of converting it into a 'destination' hostel. He and a little guy called Nick worked with a small team right through the winter. They opened in May the following year, well ahead of time for all the summer festivals, and the first backpackers started pouring in as if on tap. A stylish hand-painted sign (by me) welcomed them to the

**HOSTEL. JUNCTION. STREET.**

He'd wanted to call it 'The Happy Aussie Hostel'. Keep it simple, I said. It's not about you anyway, it's about Junction Street, Leith, the Shore, Edinburgh history. He looked a bit taken aback but went along with it. I did the artwork and design inside, framed some classy old photos of Leith, made the place atmospheric, in keeping with its Gothic character.

But I didn't like being inside the building. I was always shivering, the walls gave off a damp chill, like in a graveyard.

And like in a graveyard, I felt a presence there. It wasn't a living thing, but it was always there. Even after they'd done it up and Jackson was happily busy as manager and general runabout man at the hostel, befriending all the guests, I felt uneasy about the building. I kept looking at it from the bedroom window. Some nights, the white moon was turned towards it, like a blind marbled eye. At dusk, the unusual inlaid arch of the façade made the building look like a gaping maw against the grubby pink sky. No matter how full it was – and in summer it was chocka with young backpackers and ageing hippies – from our windows it always looked derelict.

Jackson was too busy to take an interest in its history and he wasn't superstitious. Typically Australian. But I had a close look at the building. It was rich in small, eclectic detail. It had little fat cherubic stone-heads grinning at you, and on one wall, between two such heads, was carved a faded INFANT. The year 1798 was carved on another wall, and on yet another part of the outer building, there was the small carved figure of a robed man, a priest or doctor, holding a book, with a few faded carved letters in Latin beneath, which I couldn't decipher.

Nobody in the neighbourhood knew much about the building, except that it had been in a fire, but nobody knew when, and that it had been derelict in their living memory. Dan muttered something about a Victorian orphanage, or maybe a boarding school, but I didn't trust a word Dan said. I thought about looking it up in the Leith archives, but just then, I had several portrait commissions, and got too busy to follow it up.

I recall a few small incidents though. There was the time when I was doing an all-nighter and Jackson came back from the hostel. These were my happiest times – painting high up near the pigeons and waiting for him. He didn't kiss me, which was unlike him. He walked right past me and stood at the window.

'You know,' he said, 'this place gets on my tits sometimes. There are doors in there which don't open, you know?'

I looked up from the easel, 'How do you mean?'

'I mean, they don't open. They're not locked, they just... won't open. I can't explain it. Me and Nick had to kick in a few of them tonight, 'cause we thought something bad might be going on in the room. But no – we just woke up a whole lot of punters who thought the ceiling was crashing down on them. We felt like idiots. They hadn't even locked the door. It just... I don't know. It's happened before. Some-times they won't open from *either* side. It's like a wall. It's like being walled in.'

What could I say? I knew nothing about doors. He was the one who'd done ten years of bridge-building and blowing-up.

'You need to get more sleep and stop worrying,' I said, which was worse than saying nothing.

There were a few more occasions like this, when inex-plicable things happened in the building. Increasingly, it was things going missing. Obviously there could be thieves among the long-term residents - some of whom were frankly creepy. But things went missing from locked rooms with windows so high and narrow that even a small gargoyle couldn't get in if it came to life on the side of the building. Things went missing before Jackson's eyes, he said, and Nick's too. There would be a wad of banknotes on the desk, you'd turn around to fetch something, and next thing – the cash would be gone. Other things too – clothes, tooth-brushes, even a TV set disappeared overnight. And worthless things too, like chairs, dirty socks, entire baskets of laundry.

'Well it's Scotland, what do you expect in the land of thieves and penny-pinchers,' Dan said once. 'You'll probably find all that stuff in Cash Converters round the corner.'

Then he declared that the place was haunted. He was round at ours for a drink with his latest squeeze, and wear-ing a tuxedo for some reason.

'We should hike the prices, eh Jacks? Edinburgh's first haunted hostel! People love this shit. What do you think?' He turned to the girl.

'Not much,' she said sweetly. I should have been hon-est too, with Jackson. I should have asked him to quit the hostel then, and do something else. But I didn't, I was happy he wasn't running up and down Arthur's Seat, like a maniac. I was proud of him, and he too was proud. One of my portraits, of the old Polish artist in Krakow, done from photos, was selected for the BP portrait award exhibition in the National Portrait Gallery. Several big commissions had followed.

But Jackson never sat for me. He never let me do even as much as a sketch of him. 'Nah,' he said, 'I've got an ugly mug. Paint someone with real personality.' He hated being photographed too. I gave up insisting after a while.

It was in the last ten months that Leon checked into the hostel, and took up a bunk indefinitely. He was an ex-junky from Marseille. He was about 45 but looked 60, with a sour face. But Jackson liked him, so I humoured him. Leon was often round at our flat until all hours of the night, smoking and philosophising, and watching me paint. I asked him how he'd ended up in Edinburgh.

'Oh, you know, I came to see the Sex Pistols in London twenty years ago and never left.' He was a bit vague on why he'd left London, but he had some great stories about working in a mortuary as an anatomical technician.

'You get £50 per body. Once, we went for one body, but found two. Father and daughter. Bingo! She died of a botched-up abortion, and he rolled her up in a carpet. Then he had a heart attack. I got attached to them, dunno why, but it was like that: you get attached to some bodies. You're sad when you open the fridge at work one day and they're not there - 'cause the family claimed them.'

Leon was always trying to get me to visit some tucked-away 'treasure-trove' of a cemetery. I never went. Jackson joked with him that he should have been around at the time of the body-snatchers Burke and Hare, *then* he would have been in business.

And so, when Jackson and I finally managed to get a bit of time away from our busy life in Edinburgh, it seemed natural for Jackson to offer our flat to Leon to house-sit. We were going to spend January 2009 in Australia, see Jackson's family, get a bit of sun on our pale Scottish skins.

Jackson's father had killed himself when Jackson was a boy, something he'd never told me. His mother seemed to want to tell me other things too.

Then, two weeks into our holiday, we got a phone-call from Nick. Our flat had been gutted, Leon had vanished, and 'weird shit' was happening at the hostel. We flew back, and a shrill voice was going off in my head- 'I knew it, I knew it.'

We got back just in time to see the police on the river-banks below the Junction Street bridge. They wore yellow overcoats and had dogs with them. It was raining.

Our flat was covered in cigarette butts and ash, and everything he thought was valuable was gone. Not that we had much. My paintings were intact though. I fell on my knees in tearful relief and shouted 'Thank you, God, even though I don't believe in you, thank you!' Leon clearly had no faith in my art, otherwise he would have sold it. I guess it wasn't dead enough for him. All our photos from the last six years, starting with Krakow, were gone with the computer.

Jackson went across to the hostel. It wasn't doors this time, or things gone missing, it was people. People had gone 'missing'.

'What do you mean, *missing*,' I said. My relief at find-ing my paintings untouched made me more forceful. 'You mean like that cunt Leon, gone with our stuff without leav-ing a forwarding address?'

'No, I mean like the wee daughter of a Canadian couple staying with us. She was there in her bunk in the night, and in the morning she wasn't. Missing three days now. Like the two Israeli guys who left all their stuff on their beds, every-thing – passports, money, cameras, all their shit – and just vanished a week ago. Like the Spanish girl who was last seen last week. *That kind of missing.*' He had that blank look in his eyes, the look I dreaded. 'The cops are digging all over the place. They've looked into our accounts. Dan's freaking out.'

Dan was freaking out because their accounts were dodgy. After that, everything happened fast. Leon was tracked down in a Belfast hostel and arrested, on charges of kidnap and murder. But he was eventually charged only with the theft from our flat and possession of drugs. None of the missing people were found, dead or alive. The police found nothing. Then the hostel was closed down indefinitely, not just because the missing tourists were all over the national papers, but because under scrutiny, various structural hazards were discovered. Plus the fact that Dan and Jackson had registered it as a 'charity'.

The blank look in Jackson's eyes returned for good, and he started running again, for hours every day, and always with his army rucksack. I tried to talk to him but he was too restless for that. He wouldn't make love to me anymore, just clutch me and shiver. I'd wake in the night to find he wasn't there, and I knew where he was by checking his carefully labelled key-hooks in our hallway: the keys to the hostel were missing. He was there, across the street. The first night this happened, I went across and saw him in the main hall. He was sitting there in the dark, slumped like a pile of laundry among old mattresses. He didn't see me, and I didn't say anything, I just went back to the flat and cried myself to sleep. When I mentioned seeing a doctor, he said he was just taking time out and claimed that the hostel hadn't been a big deal to him.

It was in the summer, when cats were mating on the roof, that he went missing. The authorities had no record of him leaving the country. All he'd taken was his rucksack. No money was withdrawn from our joint account, but Nick told me that Jackson kept all the cash from the hostel – tens of thousands of pounds – in big glass jars which he stored somewhere in a secret place, Nick didn't know where, or at least didn't say. Then Nick went abroad and I didn't see him until last month when he came by sporting a traveller's beard. He said something about seeing Jackson in Manila, where he was now running a hostel called The Happy Aussie, and living with some local woman. He tried to show me a photo, but I really wasn't interested, and anyway the photo showed some ugly savage with long greasy hair and beard. I told Nick not to come back, I might have yelled. Jackson, with his innocence and generosity, attracted the likes of him and Leon, and they leeched off him.

A year has gone since Jackson went missing.

'You're like that woman from *Breaking the Waves*,' one friend said. 'A bloody martyr. And that bastard cleared off without even saying goodbye.'

Some said I'd turned eccentric, which makes me laugh.

'You should be looking for those money jars of his. If he hasn't gone away, the jars will be there!' someone else said. But that's his money, wherever it is. There's enough in our joint account to keep me going for a bit longer. Other friends said I should go back to painting, that it would cure me.

But I am painting, people, it's just that I'm not showing it to anyone yet. It's a huge project.

(I'm through with portraits of course, portraits are for sissies, though they were a very good earner and it hurts to turn commissions away.)

And I don't have leprosy, people, I'm just living in Junction Street, across from a derelict building which used to be a hostel, and before that, a hospice damaged in a fire, and before that, a boarding school, and before that an orphanage, and before that a meat-packing hall. And always, always, people went missing, which is why it kept closing down.

How do I know this? Because I looked it up in the Leith archives, where every single building's history is listed, with grim Scottish meticulousness. But I also know it because I can always rely on my dreams to tell me what's going on. Dreams are out of time.

You see, Leon was just a small-time degenerate, nothing more. The building is where the real crimes are. They are crimes of time. Impersonal crimes. It's a tear in the fabric of time, this building, and its out-of-joint jaws crunch you up. It takes revenge on those who tamper with it. It feeds on human lives. The missing people are all trapped in there, behind doors that won't open – not just Jackson, not just the Canadian girl and the Israelis, but those gone missing before, in previous incarnations of the building. They're all walled in, the infants, the sick, the butchers in their stained aprons. I've seen it clearly and beyond any doubt. There is a room in the building, upstairs, where that crucifix-shaped window is...

But it will all become clear when I finish the paintings. And I'm not done yet.

With each brush-stroke, I'm getting closer to Jackson. I know he's waiting for me to let him out. I don't want to freak anyone out by telling them how at night, when I sit at my bedroom window to smoke, from the cross-shaped window at the top of the hostel I hear a faint strumming. It makes sense, because I know what I know. Some places contain our destiny, and there's no point denying it.

Recently, work has started on the building again. Men came and put scaffolding all over it, and although I still have the keys, I'm scared that I'll run out of time before I complete my project. Some nights, when the wind rushes in from the ocean, the plastic sheets of the scaffolding flap so hard against the stone that I can't hear the guitar anymore. And on those nights I feel so alone, it's as if my soul is rattling inside one of those empty Polish gherkin tins, the ones you see kicked by the wind down the corridor of Leith Walk, which comes from nowhere and leads nowhere except out to the leaden sea of the north. All the way to Norway.

# Where Things Are Happening

## Micaela Maftei

*Micaela Maftei* (signature)

For three long years, there was summer in Guthrie, where it was very hot, and winter in Aberdeen, where it was very cold. The weather was very bad. It rained much more than it ought to, she thought every day as she hunched her shoulders against the wind and tried in vain to shield her shins from the splashing of cars.

Annabel lived in a three room flat with a hotplate at one end and a toilet at the other. The bed was in the middle. She drank endless cups of tea and sat surrounded by books in an ancient pea green plastic-covered armchair that had come with the flat. The plastic was cold until her body warmed it and then it became sweaty and sticky. Apart from the hotplate, there was one other source of warmth, a gas heater made of leaping orange bars of flame that ate 50p pieces at an alarming rate and scorched the two feet directly in front of it without warming anything else. Until about November, she wore socks to bed and put on a third sweater when she got home from school. But when the winter truly started she would take her duvet off her bed and wear it like a cape. She would sit in the armchair in silence for hours, reading, thinking, once in a while crying. Whenever she got up to go to the bathroom she would fold the duvet over itself so that when she returned she could slide back in it like a potato in its jacket, pulling in her legs and letting only her wide, sad face out of the white cotton confines.

Unless she went out, she would go to bed early; changing into her pajamas under the covers. Every morning there was a warm Annabel-sized island stranded in an ocean of freezing damp air. Her family sent her an electric blanket, a package that Annabel could see had cost almost as much as

an entire weekly bread delivery, and in her excitement she
mixed up the transformers and adaptors and exploded the
thing so it sparked and puffed smoke and fell out of her
hands dead.

Going out meant she didn't need to feed coins into the
heater but it also meant she had to buy something usually
more expensive. She would sit in the pub with her classmates and sip orange juice that tasted like old grapefruits.
Invariably, one or more of them would buy packets of crisps
and gut them open on the sticky tables, sweeping a fingertip
over the greasy crumbs in the creases of the bag and licking
them off after demolishing the rest of the crisps. Many of
them were from Glasgow and acted like this was a personality trait. Some were from Aberdeen and didn't notice the tone
they adopted whenever they talked about the place. One
night one of the boys asked if she felt like a shag and called
her a cunty one when she said she didn't. His scrawny neck,
hideously white and knobby like a bone, stuck out of the
gaping, stretched collar of his t-shirt and bobbed up and
down angrily when she refused him. Near the base it was
dotted with pimples.

Sometimes one of their professors, Leonard, would
come to the pub with them. He was from London, which
everyone else seemed to know instinctively. She made the
mistake of assuming he was from Aberdeen and they crowed
with laughter and asked if she'd ever heard the man speak.
They all liked him because he was young and would occasionally buy them drinks. He'd gone to Cambridge and was
mocked for it out of earshot. When Annabel suggested this
was jealousy, they insisted they'd rather die than be one of
those types. Everyone said he was very young to be a tutor
and she had to agree. She couldn't get used to the idea of
drinking in a bar with a teacher and calling him by his first
name.

And then one day it would be over. By the time she left
there had usually been a few days of mild weather in Aberdeen, when everyone called in sick to work and sat on the
grass, starting to drink at eleven and getting up every so

often to kick a ball around. The men would take their shirts off to boil themselves red in the weak April sunshine and the girls would reveal white bellies and fat little side-breasts squeezing out of tops bought too small. But she never saw any real summer and, from what she heard, there never would be any. Summer meant home, meant Canada. Her older brother would pick her up from the air-conditioned corridors of the Toronto airport. She liked to linger in the city as long as she could, pretending that she lived there and could take the subway home instead of driving with Doug out to where their parents lived.

Her brother would take her for lunch somewhere downtown and grumble about parking and the price of a beer, wondering how people could stand living like this, while Annabel watched the sway of people on the streets, stared at apartments crammed on top of variety stores and in old warehouses, thought about living here with a gorgeous boyfriend who did something interesting like photography. The plan had been to move here after high school and let her real life begin. Then her mother's church group gave her a scholarship in the name of some doddering old woman who'd come over on a boat and left behind enough money after her weekly tins of tuna to send a congregation girl away to school in the town she'd left decades ago. Her mother told her Toronto would always be overpriced and down the high-way for her to waste her youth on and told her to pack her bags, acting as though they'd all won the lottery.

Her first summer back, she'd started crying over lunch with her brother. They were eating Thai food on a patio. The sun was on her back and she could hear reggae music coming from somewhere behind her. Everyone's body was so beautiful she couldn't stand it, and no one was perched on a fire hydrant drinking cheap beer or beating each other up in the streets before throwing up messes of undercooked fat white chips.

"What's the matter with you?"

"This is where I'm supposed to be, Doug."

"This place is a rip-off. This Coke cost three-fifty."

"Look how cool and happy everyone looks."

"Annie, these people are morons. Anyway, Dad showed me some pictures of where you live now. That's a nice castle."

This only made her cry harder. "It's the boonies," she wailed. "This is where things are happening."

He shrugged and slurped on his three-fifty Coke. "I knew it was a waste of money to send you anywhere." Now that Dad was on disability, Doug was taking over more and more of the store and in his opinion, which he took every opportunity to repeat, his sister's education was a useless and risky expense.

The drive home took two or three hours, depending on the traffic. Her family owned a rest stop that sold cheeseburgers and onion rings and calendars and ceramic mugs and inauthentic maple fudge. It was on the side of the highway and cars stopped on their way to and from cottage country. The cars that stopped usually had children in them who got what they wanted by screaming. The women all seemed blonde, even when they weren't blonde, and everyone complained about the price of gas and bickered over what to feed their kids. The mothers would poke the bulging plastic-wrapped muffins with a doubtful finger and then buy the small glass bottles of juice Doug called retard nectar.

After that first lunch in the city, there would be no more Toronto until it was time to fly back at the beginning of September. She would work at the rest stop every day and once in a while see her old high school friends. The second summer she'd spent far less time with them than the first summer, and the third summer she only saw them a few times. Not only was she usually tired after working all day, but it wasn't easy to borrow the car. And whenever she did meet up with them she was weirdly anxious. None of them went to university, although a few took courses at the community college. They always asked bizarre questions about Aberdeen and it was hard to explain that she didn't want to talk about it, that she was sick of talking about how you couldn't get cream for your coffee or that people going to soccer games were seated according to what team they were cheering for. They all seemed to think she was living in the big city and it did no good to remind them of the truth.

The rest stop was endlessly busy and before noon she would be streaked with sweat and able to smell the air conditioning on the bodies of the people who came in and asked her where they sourced their meat from and if their hamburgers were organic. She would tan in less than a week, pulling flats of pop and juice off the delivery truck, unwinding the garden hose to water the buckets of geraniums that, according to her mother, attracted customers. She would eat behind the door to the small kitchen, leftover onion rings that had been re-fried too many times to sell and cartons of milk that were close to expiry. She was allowed to read the magazines if her fingers were clean and she didn't bend the pages. At night she would have dinner standing up in front of the fridge, eating out of Tupperware because she was too tired to get out a clean bowl.

And now, finally, it was the beginning of the fourth and final year. This year she had managed to get Doug to drive her down early in the morning; her flight wasn't until night-time. It was close to forty degrees and it hadn't rained in weeks. The air was heavy and hazy – everything in the distance seemed gritty and silvery at the same time. To compensate for wasting his entire day in the city she had taken his night shifts for the past two weeks. Sometimes whole families came in at night, but usually the night shift meant pouring extra-large coffees for haggard-looking single men driving up to meet the rest of their families. Every so often one of the men would watch her stir his coffee and fit the plastic lid on before talking to her.

"Oh, you go to university? Good for you. Whereabouts?"

Most of them didn't know where Aberdeen was, but pretended to. Those that did would look at her in surprise, almost suspicious.

"In England?"

"Scotland. Next to England."

"Same thing," they would say. Or, "well how about that." Or, "bet it's rainy as hell over there." And once, "why's a pretty little thing like you want to go so far away for?" And to all of them she said "Dollar forty-five please," without looking up.

Doug had complained the whole drive down. "Why would you want to spend the whole day walking around in this weather? It's goddamn hot. Where the hell am I going to put the car? Jesus, Annie, you'd think you'd learn a thing or two with all this school." In the end he dropped her off downtown and told her he'd meet her for dinner. He was off to catch up with an old friend from high school who'd moved out here for god knows what reason but at least probably had a driveway to put the car in. She wandered the city all day, elated, walking for hours even when her jeans got stiff and sticky. At dinner, Doug was fuming. His friend had no driveway and lived in a sixteenth-floor condo.

They ate dinner at a Vietnamese restaurant in Chinatown. The streets were teeming with people walking over the slimy remains of that day's vegetable sales. Doug asked the waitress for a fork. Couples walked past glued together by the heat, shining where they were naked. The sun was setting and the whole neighborhood was orange and steaming. Annabel ate spring rolls and cold noodles, watching the stop lights controlling everything.

Arriving in Scotland, Annabel was conscious of doing things for the last time. *This is the last time I will land in this country, she thought. This is the last time I will take the train in this direction. This is the last time I will bring my full suitcase into this place.*

The first time they went to the pub Leonard was there. He welcomed them back and they looked sheepish, waiting to see if, not being their tutor any longer, he would still buy them drinks. Annabel was one of the lucky winners and she chatted to him for a short while, astounded when she realized they'd been talking for well over an hour. When he left he looked closely at her.

The next time he came to the pub and bought her another drink, it felt like a done thing. She went outside the pub with him for a cigarette even though she rarely smoked.

"Home to the city for summer?"

"What?"

"Aren't you from Toronto?"

"Yes," she said.

"I expect it's a bit livelier than here," he said.

"Yes," she said.

"Well then."

"You went to a small town for school too, didn't you?"

"What do you mean?"

"Didn't you go to Cambridge? That's a small town."

He looked at her curiously. "I suppose it is a small town."

"Would you like to go somewhere else?" he asked her when they finished their cigarettes.

"No, thanks. Everything's the same around here."

"Shall I buy you another drink inside, then?"

"No, thanks."

"Shall we go for a bit of a walk?"

She was outraged at how certain he appeared, forgetting that she'd felt an inevitability about it herself.

"Have you been to London?"

"No."

"It's quite expensive."

She sighed. "Then you must be rich."

He laughed uncomfortably. "Just half the family. But the half that counts. You might know a bit about that yourself, flying halfway round the world to do an arts degree."

She was stunned. "I guess I do," she lied, before adding, "I thought British people never talked about money." She didn't know where this impression had come from. In fact, her classmates were only too glad to compare prices and wages.

He laughed uncomfortably again.

"I'm American," he said. "Born there. We moved before I could talk. So I sound like this. But only half of us moved."

"The half that doesn't count?" guessed Annabel. He

grinned.

"The rich are different from you and me," he said, as if this was an explanation.

"I guess they have more money," she said, wondering if that sounded rude. He looked at her curiously again and she worried she'd sounded foolish.

"I've spent time in Toronto," he said abruptly. "I went for a year when I was younger, and I've gone to conferences and things here and there. Bit of a toddler of a city, don't you think? Doesn't know quite how big or small it is, or what to do with itself."

"No. I think it's amazing," she said. "I should go back. My friends are waiting."

"Of course, of course they are. Let's spend some time together, Annabel. Your papers last year showed a lot of promise." He said these three sentences as though they bore some relation to each other.

Leonard lived in a flat entirely different from hers, with heat and matching cutlery and a duvet that always stayed on top of the bed. Leonard liked to tell stories about people he used to know that bored Annabel to tears because it seemed all he'd ever done with these people was sit around and put down other people. Once in a while he talked about his family and growing up. There was the important half, and the half with money. Those were the two different halves of the Leonard-whole. Annabel never talked about her family or growing up, or how she wasn't divided into halves, unless there was a highway half and a lying-by-omission half. Periodically she would slip up and make some allusion to home and he would tell her the thing he liked most about Canadians was how their provincial ways always seemed like modesty. They would both laugh.

Then it was Christmas. There was never enough money to fly home more than once a year. The first year Annabel had sat in her flat, dumb with grief under the duvet. Her family called at an odd hour on Christmas Day, clamouring for space on the other end of the line before suddenly hanging up because of the cost. The following two years she had been invited to two different classmates' houses. She brought wine and biscuits and both years she received a scarf from the two different mothers, an inoffensive color that matched everything. One scarf was of significantly higher quality than the other.

At the beginning of December, Leonard asked if she wanted to come with him to see his family for Christmas.

"To meet half the family?" she asked, "no, thanks."

"Why not?"

"I don't feel like going to London," she lied.

"I'm not going to London. Not that half."

The other half was in Manhattan.

"I don't think so," she said.

"You can't just sit here all break," he said, with enough certainty that she began to doubt whether she had actually spent the past three Christmas breaks just sitting here. After the third time he asked, she closed her eyes and told him she didn't want to spend the money for the ticket. He burst out laughing. "Jesus, who cares about the *ticket*? I'll buy them both tomorrow."

In the air, Annabel watched the plane's path across the television screen. She could see Toronto on the map, close to the red star that was their destination. Leonard said they could drive up for a day or so to see her family, which Annabel knew was impossible. So she told him her family always went somewhere warm for the holidays.

They took a cab into the city. Annabel was fixated by the meter, thrilled and horrified by the numbers. Half of Leonard's family lived in an apartment next to the park. There was no snow and the streets looked dirty in the brilliant sunshine. After the low, dark sky in Aberdeen, she stared up in amazement. The elevator opened directly into the apartment. A woman walked up and Annabel stuck out her hand. Leonard took her hand in his and the woman picked up Annabel's bag, smiled, and walked away with it. Another woman with silver hair came around the corner and Leonard dropped Annabel's hand. The silver-haired woman spent a long time looking into Annabel's face and a longer time looking into Leonard's. Finally she clasped her hands together and spoke.

"Leonard. You're here. You must be Annabel." She continued looking at Leonard when she said the final sentence and Annabel couldn't stop herself from tittering. She stuck out her hand again and the woman looked at it, surprised. "Annabel," said Leonard, "this is my stepmother, Beverly." "Hello, Beverly," said Annabel, and the woman raised her eyebrows slightly and smiled brilliantly. "Hello, darling," she responded, and closed both her hands around Annabel's. "Mary took your bag to your room. How was your flight?" she began leading her down the hall, and Annabel looked over her shoulder at Leonard, who was shouldering his own bag but wasn't walking with them.

"Bev," he called out, but Beverly pretended not to have heard him and continued leading Annabel away.

"Fine," Annabel answered distractedly, wondering why Leonard wasn't following them, "the flight was fine."

The apartment had long hallways and was flooded with sunlight. The floors were polished wood and some of the paintings in the hallways hung below their own little lamps. They turned a corner and Beverly opened a door. The room had a small bed and dresser. There were recent magazines on the bedside table and a vase of fresh flowers on the windowsill. Annabel's bag was already next to the bed.

"This is your room, dear," said Beverly. Annabel stared. "Where's Leonard's room?" she asked, and for some reason it came out as a whisper. Beverly smiled. "No doubt he'll show it to you later. Lunch is at one."

"Where's Leonard?" Annabel asked.

"I'll ask Mary to find him," Beverly assured her. She swept out of the room.

Annabel walked to the window and looked out. An endless stream of cars, most of them taxis, poured down the street. People pushed past each other on the sidewalks. Annabel looked at her watch. It was quarter past eleven. What was she supposed to do until one? Leonard appeared in the doorway.

"What's going on?"

"What do you mean?"

"How come we aren't sleeping in the same room?"

"Because we can't," he said.

"Where's your father?" she asked.

Leonard shrugged. "At the office? We'll probably see him at lunch."

"What are we supposed to do until then?"

He shrugged again. "Settle in."

"Where are you sleeping?"

He nodded his head out the door, "my room is down the other hall."

"Can I see it?"

"Now?"

"Yeah, now."

He shrugged again and walked out. She followed him out of the room and through the apartment. There actually was a whole other hallway. They passed an enormous white kitchen with no one in it, and a room filled with dark wood and books. Annabel spied a photo of Leonard as a child on one of the walls. He was wearing a suit and tie.

Leonard's room was much bigger than hers. There were full bookcases lining the walls and his windows looked onto the park. He stood in the doorway while she looked around. She picked up a framed picture of Leonard next to two other people in graduation robes. They were standing next to a stone wall in sunlight.

"Is this from Cambridge?"

He nodded.

"Where's your diploma?" she asked.

He shrugged. "It's probably in London, actually. I can't remember."

"You can't *remember*?" Annabel and Doug's high school graduation certificates were framed and hanging in the living room back home. Her mother had already bought a new, expensive frame for the diploma she was going to get in a few months. She opened his closet, which was filled with clothes. "I thought you were never here," she said. "I thought all your stuff is in London."

"It is. This is just some old stuff." He came and stood beside her as if to remind himself of what was in there. They stared into the closet; a few seconds later there was a noise down the hall and Leonard jumped. Annabel laughed.

"Relax," she told him, and reached nervously for his tucked-in shirt. He stiffened.

"That's not a good idea," he told her, and took a step back.

"Just close the door," she said.

"No, really."

"What the hell else are we supposed to do until lunch?" she asked, half-joking.

"Why don't you go unpack?" he said brightly, pleased at the idea. He walked to the doorway and waited. Annabel cleared her throat.

"Alright," she said evenly, "I guess I'll see you at lunch then."

"Sounds great," Leonard said. "It'll be fine."

"What will be fine?"

"Oh, well, everything I guess." He nodded vigorously. "It'll be fine," he repeated.

Annabel left the room and Leonard closed the door halfway behind her. She walked back down the hall and passed the kitchen again. It was still empty. She walked in and looked around. The fridge was smaller than her arm span, but not by much. Annabel walked up to the window and saw another door leading out of the kitchen. Thinking it led back to the hallway, she pushed it open. It was another room altogether and someone was talking in it.

"Who knows, he's always been a little off," the voice said.

"There's no point talking about it," replied someone else, "did I mention she tried to shake my hand? Did I mention that?"

"He has completely lost his brains," said the first voice. "If they think I'm working overtime for this they can find someone else. It's not just Christmas for them, you know. My nephew's coming to town."

"If you just lay down some newspaper and give her fresh water every day she'll probably be fine," said the second voice. Both laughed. One of them sighed.

"If this one has any crazy food rules, I'm finding another job."

"I think she'll be happy enough to get a bite to eat."

"Completely lost his brains. Why does he still bother coming here? What's he trying to prove?"

Annabel closed the door. She stood in front of it for a moment, then turned and walked out the way she'd come. She padded down the hallway until she found her own room again. It was almost noon. She had no American money, but she had her credit card and she had carried her own plane ticket. She took two of the magazines off the nightstand and tucked them into her bag. She tiptoed down the hallway, wondering where on earth everyone was. She prayed the elevator button wouldn't make any noise when she pressed it. As the doors closed on her view of the apartment, she thought she heard a voice and footsteps coming towards her. On the street, she walked blindly until she reached a corner and then stuck out her hand.

At the bus station she sat on an empty bench and watched a man sleep under a bank of public telephones. None of the telephones were in service, which she knew because she had tried to use them to call her parents' house while she waited for the bus. She waited over two hours for the only bus of the day. She would be in Guthrie around midnight. It was silly to feel this way, since she was in another country after all, but as soon as the bus left the city and started rumbling down the long empty highway, she felt right at home.

# A Snake Drinks Water and Makes Poison, A Cow Drinks Water and Makes Milk

*All the best,*

## Kevin MacNeil

It's not just about 'Why are we here?' but 'Who can understand this universe - when it's a universe of the impossible?' The notion of what is going to happen crosses no human mind here, now. It is a lovely morning, a morning lazily vibrant in sunlight. Holidaymakers relax under an already hot sun, they make blurred foreign chat about yesterday's festivities, some go for a refreshing swim and others, backpackers in particular, picnic under the palm trees. A long-haired man in a purple thong crack-splutters open a tin of beer, licks at its froth, then tilts it back at a high angle, guzzling it in one, straight down the throat. His breakfast. Children play, buoyed by a natural seaside exuberance, and the locals ready their fishing equipment or hawk trinkets to the susceptible. In the final analysis we all are.

Only the elephants have a sense of it, a disquieting clairvoyance that compels them to wrench free of their chains and bulldoze their way into the forest behind. A number of these sagacious stramashing beasts carry alarmed tourists on their back. Scared as they are, these tourists will later be grateful that this small measure was the worst of the fear they had to endure today.

I catch a glimpse of one elephant stomping along, trumpeting like he's practising for the Day of Judgement and he has such a worried look on his face that I laugh out loud – at the elephant because it looks worried, and at myself for thinking Oh look, there goes a worried elephant.

As the elephants barge daintily on huge wafting feet into that chattering forest behind the hotels, birds twirp melodious, anxious tunes, a sweet and dissonant cacophony

counterpointing the chugging of boat engines. It reminds me
of how the drunken jazz of foreign birdsong had this morning bubbled up through my nightmare. Something about
Kimi, and the reason she became my ex. The details fade
even as I recall them, but an indelible sense of sadness fills
my mind, tainting the morning.

It's six days and one weird plane ride since I saw, and
then no longer saw, Kimi. Trying to escape my mind. Everywhere I go, here it is. Too much me to be of use to me.
Seething with anxieties. I deserve it. I can't stand it. My mind
is, as the Canadian Gaels used to say, restless as a frog eating lightning.

Hmm. Restless like the elephants and birds are today.

I maintain my passive ways. It's a kind of penance.

Life is always around a labyrinth-corner, teasing you
like a sad-smiling girl. '*La vraie vie est absente. Nous ne
sommes pas au monde,*' said hardcore, sense-disordered,
heaven-sent, hell-bound poet Rimbaud. 'True life is elsewhere. We are not in the world.'

Sometimes, docile in an urban reverie, while people
mill around and the streets bustle with laughter and anger, I
feel like a ghost. Might as well fade away. Do even ghosts
fade in time?

Kimi. Memories. Your luminous name is enough. Skin-
bristling. Hurt. Your benign haunting in my mind shall always tingle and glow.

How could I -?

Even here, on the early beach, where I lay a scratchy
towel on the soft sand, mid-way between the hotel than the
sea, I am an observer, one who feels so insignificant he won-
ders if anyone else here can see him.

Of course they can. They choose not to.

I deserve it, I do.

The scent of sea-salt and diesel (from the ever-droning
longtail taxi boats) reminds me of ferry journeys from my
home island to the mainland, groggy mornings on the way
back to student life in Edinburgh.

There's a lovely deep blue sky and when you gather

some of the fine warm yellow sand it flows through your fingers with a shivery, sensual pleasure. Write injuries in sand, the French say, kindnesses in marble. Sand can be a window, concrete, a water filter. Marble can be toothpaste, concrete, a sculpture or building.

I am building a Taj Mahal on quicksand. *La vraie vie est absente.*

A great many people – French, Swedish, American, German, English and so on - are holidaying here. I hadn't realized so many people chose to spend their Christmas in places like this. Perhaps that's because most people I know don't have much money and those who do have money often spend it on cultivating their eccentricities.

The beach is a little quieter than it was yesterday since, Christmas being Christmas and tourists being tourists, hangovers are doubtless battering many heads back onto their downy white hotel pillows.

I mull over the Christian contemplation of the hangover, famously recounted by one of my primary school teachers before multi-faith-ism was the norm in Scottish island schools. Proverbs 23. I later memorized it: "Who hath woe? Who hath sorrow? Who hath contentions? Who hath babbling? Who hath wounds without cause? Who hath redness of eyes? They that tarry long at the wine; they that go to seek mixed wine. Look not thou upon the wine when it is red, when it giveth his colour in the cup, when it moveth itself aright. At last it biteth like a serpent, and stingeth like an adder. Thine eyes shall behold strange women, and thine heart shall utter perverse things. Yeah, thou shalt be as he that lieth down in the midst of the sea, or as he that lieth upon the top of a mast."

Seonaidh Ramone once gave me a T-shirt he'd bought in New York City. And purchased, I later learned, from a junkie who had *literally* given him the shirt off his back. That's not why I refused to wear it though. The shirt read in tiny script:

*"Christianity: The belief that a cosmic Jewish Zombie who was his own father can make you live forever if you symbolically eat his flesh and telepathically tell him you accept him as your master, so he can remove an evil force from your soul that is present in humanity because a rib-woman was convinced by a talking snake to munch on an apple from a magical tree."*

I'd never seen that quotation before, though I've come across it a few times since. I agonize over big questions, small details. I think too much. I do not think enough. I wonder who and why I am. We are hardwired to ask these questions. And, I suspect, hardwired to answer them.

I confess a soft spot for Christmas Carols, whose naïve and poignant melodies reach under my defences with a sentimentality that would make Tiny Tim boke. Two night ago, three blonde little girls swanned past my hotel singing an earnest, harmonious 'O Little Town of Bethlehem' and that lovely innocent human melody annihilated all anxiety in my mind and set a grateful tear wobbling in my eye.

> Above thy deep and dreamless sleep,
> The silent stars go by;
> Yet in thy dark streets shineth
> The everlasting Light;
> The hopes and fears of all the years
> Are met in thee tonight.
>
> Where children pure and happy
> Pray to the blessed Child,
> Where misery cries out to thee,
> Son of the mother mild;
> Where charity stands watching
> And faith holds wide the door,
> The dark night wakes, the glory breaks,
> And Christmas comes once more.

I strained to hear them as they receded, their pure lips carrying hope, fear, charity, faith and redemption into the night. Odd that they would go carol-singing in Thailand, but kids will always be kids. Bless 'em.

As *their* dark night trailed into the actual dark night and glory vaguely broke, Christmas itself vanished.

I wept that night. I sent a silent prayer that Kimi, preternatural as any angel on this earth, might appear at the door and we could talk everything through and I could beg her forgiveness and I solemnly believed I could wash her feet with my tears and - Kimi, come back to me, Kimi, even when impossible -

Thunk. There was a knock at the door.

I wiped my nose on my T-shirt sleeve, opened my eyes wide.

Alert.

Nothing.

I had imagined it, thank God.

Thunk. My heart gave a fearful little leap. I got to my unsteady feet.

I started formulating an incoherent prayer as I reached out to open the door.

Standing there was a crazy-eyed man reeking of cheap local whisky. He looked a little like me. He gave a sharp splutter of laughter.

'You,' he said, jabbing an index finger at my chest, 'are not my wife.' His accent was London. Cockney.

I had no energy for politeness. 'No,' I said. 'I'm not.'

'Who are you anyway - my brother?' He let loose a snottery barrage of asthmatic laughter.

'Hope not,' I said, too quiet for him to hear.

'What have you done with my wife?' He started looking around me and made to come into my room.

'Look, pal, you've got the wrong room.'

'No, you have. Two one four.'

'This is one one four. You're next floor up.'

To the drunk, surprise and serendipity lose their magic. 'So you don't have the wife?' He paused, wobbled on his feet. 'Good for you.' He grabbed my hand, shook it almost violently and grinned. 'Good for you.'

I freed my hand. 'Lift's over there,' I said, pointing.

I slammed the door shut.

'And a Merry Christmas to you, you miserable twat,' he shouted and with a farewell punch to the door he staggered off to his room, his wife, his hangover and, two days later, his death.

This is the first Christmas I haven't received a single card or present. Most people don't know where I am. I sent Kimi a text before I arrived to tell her which country I'd come to for the time being. I spent the greater part of yesterday lying on the beach here writing and wondering if I should phone Kimi. I decided not to. She made no effort to get in touch with me, but that is understandable.

It's odd, having a hot 'festive' season, all the more so since just a few days ago I was halfway up a cold Mount Fuji...

I'm lying down here on a big blue towel, wearing an inscrutable brown and white Japanese T-shirt (Kimi wouldn't tell me what it says), long brown shorts, indiscriminately coloured sandals and a fatty all-over smear of Factor 40 suncream. Scottish as ever, on my first day here I'd misjudged the sun to sun-cream ratio and by mid-afternoon my skin had flamed from papery white to crispy red. The pain, the itching, the sleep-depriving discomfort have none-the-less seemed warranted. It's early in the morning and there's an occasional teasing breeze but already I can feel the day's impending suffocation, the punishing saline heat.

I've spent my few days and evenings lying around, writing or reading or taking pensive walks among revoltingly happy couples.

Right now, by my side, I have the enigmatic, subtle Japanese pen and the haiku-perfect wee notebook Kimi gave me. She could never have guessed that, after filling one half with love poems, I'd start that intense pen, like a single-pointed mind, nuzzling inky lyrical *apologies* onto the remaining pages. Sorrowful poems that perhaps bettered their heartglowing counterparts, albeit at a cost that was - is - exorbitant.

God forgive me.

I lie down on the rough towel, wincing as my sunburn flares and weeps. The notebook and pen are positioned with a writer's natural self-consciousness beside a two-litre bottle of already-warm-but-at-least-it's-wet water. My inner voice curses me for leaving my hat at the hotel: typical useless me. I'd only just begun liking myself again when I...

The ground shakes. At first I think an elephant has stomped past right behind me. No. I blur – everything blurs – in this huge shuddering from nowhere. It's like sitting on a washing machine. Tremors. Vast tremors. God's wild heart breaking. The depth charge in my mind during one of its episodes. The water bottle trembles, my whole body rattles, the Earth itself seems to shoogle from here to Hell's outermost horizon. People's faces jolt awake with surprise and shock. A coconut falls off a tree and thumps off an Australian's head, much to his pals' lagered amusement. They insult him between bursts of laughter.

The tremor lasts a few moments and when it fades and we realize we're all okay we share confused smiles and lapse into a curious collective stillness, a happy-baffled acquiescence.

My heart beats hard. This is how it feels; the Earth has had some palpitations and then calmed herself so now everything is just fine, as it was always more or less meant to be. But my nature is not that of the good green Earth – which, in any case is three-quarters blue. Great kettle-drum beatings within my heart are shaking me, shaking me...

Deep breaths. In, hold one-thousand two-thousand three-thousand four-thousand, out. It's all going to be fine. You're fine. Worse things happen at - hey, Kimi herself, who knows, might also be fixable.

A little later, I sit up and open the water bottle, take a heavy swig, swish the lukewarm elixir round my mouth a few times. Something about this action always makes you scan your surroundings. The beach is much busier now, though I bet a fair number of people are still in their hotel-rooms, poisonheaded and remorseful. I carry on gazing around as I screw the lid back in place, watch locals peddling trinkets to tourists or fixing fishing lines. I knock the bottle over.

'Damnit!'

I pick the bottle up. The water's already seeping into both sand and towel, forming a drowned map. My fingers give a nervous shake and I drop the bottle onto the self-same damp stain.

I pick the bottle up again. 'I can't believe this.' (Talking to yourself, another writerly habit).

Something makes me glance up and standing there is an Asian girl, a little local girl staring at me with a shy smile on her lips. She's about ten years old. Maybe the fact I'm obviously foreign, speaking a funny language, talking to myself, maybe just my sheer stupid lack of coordination – who knows, but something is making her happy. I'm glad to be giving someone a reason to smile.

Feels good. Maybe I just look funny.

I smile back at her. 'It's okay, it's only water. I can just dilute what's left of it.'

She holds my gaze, grinning. She's such a cute wee thing, the more so for how bemused she looks. She turns with a twinkle back to the sea. Her long glossy black hair is tied into a ponytail that reaches the small of her back. Her two-piece bathing suit is a vivid pink.

I wonder where her parents are.

The sun is white hot, the sea luscious aquamarine.

Damn. The sunburned skin on my back and upper shoulders writhes every time I think about it. I try not to think about it, or about Kimi.

Before long the sand will be too hot to walk on barefoot. My body prickles and drips with sweat, dissolving the sun-cream's usefulness. I'll need to remember to keep reapplying it. I'm aware of my own smell, a curious mixture of the feminine peachy-keen sun-cream and the harsh animal tang of my armpits. The combined aroma makes me shudder.

Change tack.

I consider how the sun, the great sun, which sustains

life on Earth just as other stars could and perhaps should do on other planets, the sun, our solar heart, is *carcinogenic*. Even as we lie worshipping it, the sun beats down on us with cancerous waves. I sit up, sweating. I want to shake my fist at the sky: *Well aren't you the contrary Universe.*

God invents the Sun, Satan blasts it with Cancer.

Actually, the girl looked not just Asian but Eurasian. She will be beautiful when she grows up.Why is she standing there in that same spot, statue-still, staring? Maybe she isn't quite right. Staring at the sea... Wait.

*The sea that isn't there.* The sea has retreated. As if the ocean were a blanket some grumpy sea god on the other side pulled towards himself in his half-sleep.

I blink.

The sea has withdrawn. What?

Yes, the gorgeous green-blue sea has rolled away, exposing the beach, and has done so with such haste it's left fish writhing, gasping, on the naked shore. New islands of sand and coral have appeared. Soft underwater – supposedly underwater – grasses wilt in the immediate heat, cough up little creatures which flicker around in desperation.

Swimmers are screaming, out of nervous excitement or flat-out fear. Their screams are contradictory - becoming more intense yet a little quieter as the waves pull them further out to sea.

I'm not sure this is happening. Because it can't be.

The girl is transfixed; she's frozen there in the heat, staring at what my own eyes are struggling to decipher.

The sea has recoiled and is starting to bubble in the distance. Fishing boats on the horizon have begun to bob up and down.

This – this is deeply unsettling.

I almost doubt this little girl exists, I couldn't swear on any bible that the sea is really performing such an unnatural act. Or is it normal for this part of the world? Maybe at a certain time of the month, or year? An annual sudden extreme low tide? But wouldn't I have at least heard of it? Not necessarily.

Even if it can't be, I'm certain this *is* happening.

I look around. People are observing it with amazed or bemused disbelief. Some tourists are wowing, some are frowning. Phone cameras and digital cameras are raised and pointed, then laughed and/or worried at. Some people are babbling in German, some in Swedish, some in English, but their general tenor is the same. Translation: *Gasp.*

Little children – but not my wee girl – go running towards the non-sea, shrieking, their buckets and spades clattering. 'Starfish! Starfish!' screeches a little (Londoner?) boy and half a dozen kids dash towards him as he picks something up, deposits it in his bucket then runs to the impossibly far-off waves, his dogged little troop racing after him.

Local fishermen stride or jog towards the weird shore space, swinging buckets and nets. Their faces, normally smiling and calm, are animated.

What is this about?

The sun glares down. Children fill their blue, red, green, buckets with quirks of ocean life. Over there, some kids scream in excited terror as a sea creature wriggles its last moments of this life in their childish, sticky, godlike hands.

Fishermen, O-mouthed, rush from one area to another, grabbing fish and piling them into bags, buckets, nets, knotted T-shirts. Surprised at today's freakish, easy bounty. A lucky day.

Even so, I'm growing certain the older fishermen, who have not moved, are alarmed at how the sea has sucked itself horizonwards. A scattering of tourists and locals appears to be trying to revive some of the literally deserted flapping fish with water bottles and buckets. I pick up my half-empty water bottle, thinking.

I look at my girl. Her petite body is still facing away from me, but I can tell she's nervous as both her arms are now bent in a way that suggests she's biting her nails or playing with her lips.

Where are her parents? Is her father one of the fishermen?

Suddenly with a blush that flushes through my already superheated body I notice that a wee trickle of urine has escaped from her bikini bottom and is running down her leg. She angles her legs, knee to knee, big toe to big toe, and buries her head in her hands.

The pee rivulets down her leg and dribbles into the sand. She needn't be embarrassed, though, as no one has noticed.

Everyone is still beguiled by the supernatural anomaly. (Or some people, I notice, have picked up their things and started making their cautious way back to the hotels). I don't know. The departing sea looks almost Biblical. It's like a fairly convincing special effect from a blockbuster movie.

The dribble of her involuntary wee peters out. She lifts her head to see who has noticed her situation.

No one has noticed.

She swings round and I turn away to save her any embarrassment, alas not quickly enough and for just the briefest and most humiliating of moments our glances collide and an uncomfortable knowledge passes between us.

We both jolt our heads back towards the horizon. The furthest waves bubble under the sky, putting me in mind of a cauldron... At the same time the sea out there has formed a kind of swaying, bellydancing cliff which flashes sunlight and seems to waver and shimmy in a manner that is hallucinatory: ominous, hypnotic... weirdly beautiful.

And very, very wrong.

It's as if the whole ocean is lifting herself up, raising a wall from the horizon heavenwards.

Staring out at the rising, churning wall of white, I feel I'm losing touch with my mind, and it petrifies me because, although I usually have the sensation of being in a film – or, rather, of being that film's cameraman – I have never filmed a disaster movie before. Love and horror, yes, in the recent film 'Kimi'...

The water-wall, increasing in magnificence as it starts to draw nearer to reality, becomes all the more mesmerizing. As it nears it grows with a rush-and-roar like a light madness has begun darkening.

The fishing boats and longtail tourist boats are now making their way towards the shore. They're racing towards the shore.

It's unreal. Truly unreal.

Like watching the events of the eleventh of September three years ago, thinking *Is this actual? Is this real-life?* Knowing that certainties we had previously relied upon were collapsing into dust, into ashes. Debris falling through that crystalline blue sky like a typical New York City ticker tape parade. Then people falling. And afterwards the bloody minded wash blood with blood.

This. What is happening here? As the wall-wave charges ahead, I ask myself if this is the end of the world. It's normal to have insane thoughts in insane situations.

Who or what is causing this?

What *is* this?

People on the beach begin screaming. Some yell out names, calling children back from their hunt for stranded sea creatures. Men are barking advice. Kids start crying as they pick up on the increasing atmosphere of unease and danger. Many people are simply screaming out of fear and confusion.

Their hollering rises in harmony with the gathering roar of the sea.

A tall German man spits a few words I take to be well-meaning warnings as he runs past me, spraying me with in-advertent sand. Some gritty, salty sand finds its way into my mouth and before I know what I'm doing, I've swallowed it.

I cough up gunk, realize I'm the only person who isn't standing. I get up, worried as ever that self-consciousness will make me clumsy and stupid. I wipe sand off my face and feet and put on my sandals. I pick up my notebook and put it in my pocket. Make a mental note to abandon my towel and water bottle. Many people are now running, terrified, away from the sea, towards the safety of the hotels, beach huts or bars. Now that I'm standing upright I can better un-derstand their fright. The wall of water has caught up with and battered its way through the first wave of boats. Now, speeding up, it's going to smash the next little armada. That huge wall of water barrels through even the large boats as though they're a child's balsa-wood toys.

The boats are flung, jacknifed, into the air; the bodies that had been in them, too. Like a Greek god grown petulant, the sea is throwing people around, it is smashing boats, it is surely, right before our eyes, killing people. This water – the source of our origins? – has lost any affinity it might once have had with us.

God help those at sea.

Salt rank in my mouth, salt prickly in my eyes.

The beach is losing people, one way or the other. Sure as I'm standing here in my gritty old sandals, some of those poor swimmers have perished. Most? The outrush of men, women and children from the beach is not a stampede, quite, but it's clear some individuals now regard this as a race that will determine whether they will live into a future or die.

While people push past me, I realize I am, typically, the only one brainless and passive enough to stand around doing nothing.

Except –

There's the girl in the little pink bikini. She, too, is looking out at the water, as if daring it to outstare her. I'm now certain her father is a fisherman. Is she watching him die? I'm also certain of what must be done.

I focus. Everyone else disappears, just as when Kimi was around.

I step towards her. 'Hey!' I reach out, swivel her towards me and make trusting eye contact with her. I bend down so we're at the same level. 'Forget about daddy for the moment. I, uh – this is crazy. You can't stay here, a *ghràidh*. You will die. I can't let you die, sweetie.'

'Trust me, little one. Just trust me.'

So saying, I lunge at her. I grab her. Even as I'm standing, lifting her up, she starts railing against me, kicking and punching. She wriggles like an armful of eels so I hold her tighter. The people streaming past pay no heed.

She weighs more than I expected, but taking *active* part in one of my films has given me strength. She digs her little fingernails into my back, enraging my sunburn, and I can feel her nails tearing the skin, even through my T-shirt. I'm striding away from the sea now, not daring to look back. I clench my teeth as her nails needle at my weeping sunburn. I want to howl. People mill and flow around us. The noise, the shouting, the screaming, is a horror in itself.

It occurs to me - I'm carrying her with her kicking legs wrapped about my torso, her fingers scoring my back, her glossy black hair against my neck - she can see the wave and the death it is bringing, causing. Perhaps, right now, picking out her father.

I tense my right inside forearm under her buttocks and step up the pace. Her head turns a little against my neck – good, she is choosing not to watch, just nuzzle into my neck, my poor wee darling – a fierce electric pain blazes through my neck. She bit me! Jesus. She bit through my skin. Sharp little teeth. The pain sends a shock of whiteness flashing half an instant through my eyes. I relax my grip, almost.

I cannot let her down.

Her weight on me is causing my sandals to sink heavily into the sand but I make my – our - way up the beach - even though I'd like to be sitting on the beach, waiting for the wave to receive me – penance – to cleanse me – even though I'd like to be running on my own - faster - even though - I think my neck is bleeding - she must have a dirty film of sweaty sun-cream on her lips - she's whining, almost silently - maybe she can't speak - but then even if she could I wouldn't understand her – my skin's melting – crying - I could almost welcome a dousing of water - don't think like that – aaahh - try move faster still, but - her weight - aaaaahhhh - try speed up – we're weaving - like a boxer in a fever-dream - got to get her - to my hotel - room – she's struggling - in my arms with - strength I wouldn't have believed - reminds me - strong - people sprinting – people - pushing - past – I am - part hug - part human prison –

Christ - the more – her - little - body - thrashes – the – more – tightly – I – grip - her – let us – get – through – this...
    We stumble –

    We stumble on.

# Biographies

---

**Alan Bissett** is from Falkirk. He is the author of the novels Boyracers, The Incredible Adam Spark and, most recently, Death of a Ladies' Man. His plays include Turbo Folk, The Ching Room, and his own 'one-woman show', The Moira Monologues, which is touring Scotland throughout 2010.

**Nora Chassler** grew up in NYC. She now lives in Dundee with her nine year-old daughter, her partner, and her young poodle. Her first novel, Miss Thing, was published in January 2010. She is finishing her second, Grandmother Divided by Monkey Equals Outer Space. She's Awfy No Well is a character study for her third, which is set in Dundee.

**Sophie Cooke** is an award-winning short story writer, novelist, poet, and travel writer. Her first two novels The Glass House and Under The Mountain are published by Random House in the UK, Australia, New Zealand, Canada and South Africa. She currently lives in Edinburgh.

**Jason Donald** was born in Dundee, Scotland but grew up in Pretoria, South Africa. His first novel, Choke Chain, was published by Jonathan Cape in 2009. He lives in Glasgow.

**Rodge Glass** was born in 1978, grew up in England and has mostly lived in Scotland since 1997. His first novel *No Fireworks* (Faber & Faber, 2005) was nominated for four awards. This was followed by a second novel *Hope for Newborns* (Faber & Faber, 2008) and soon after by *Alasdair Gray: A Secretary's Biography* (Bloomsbury, 2008) which won the Somerset Maugham Award for Non-Fiction 2009. He has recently been appointed a Lecturer in Creative Writing at

Strathclyde University, and is about to finish a two year post as Keith Wright Memorial Writing Fellow there. Current projects include a comic called *Dougie's War* (Freight, 2010, in collaboration with artist David Turbitt), and *Giggs Will Tear You Apart*, a novel, due to be completed in 2011.

**Kirstin Innes** won the 2008 SAC New Writers Award, and has been published in Gutter Magazine, New Writing Scotland and the EIBF anthology, Elsewhere. She has performed her work at Connect Festival, the Edinburgh International Book Festival, and on BBC Radio Scotland, and co-runs performance event Words Per Minute. As a journalist, she writes for The Scotsman, The Herald, The Independent and The List.

**Doug Johnstone** is a writer, musician and journalist based in Edinburgh. He's had two novels published by Penguin, Tombstoning and The Ossians. His next novel, Smokeheads, will be published by Faber in 2011. Doug is in several bands including Northern Alliance, who have released four critically acclaimed albums.

**Kapka Kassabova** was raised in Bulgaria and emigrated to New Zealand as a teenager. Her memoir Street Without a Name (Portobello 2008) was short-listed for the Dolman Travel Club award and Le prix du livre européen. Her poetry is published by Bloodaxe. Kapka is Royal Literary Fellow at Strathclyde University.

**Helen Lynch** has two daughters and lives in Aberdeen, where she teaches Medieval Literature at the University and plays in all-girl ceilidh band Danse McCabre. The Elephant and the Polish Question, a collection of interlinked short stories set during the collapse of Communism in Eastern Europe, was published by Bluechrome in 2009.

**Micaela Maftei** lives in Glasgow, Scotland.

**Anneliese Mackintosh**'s work has been published in various literary magazines and anthologies, as well as broadcast on BBC Radio 4. She regularly performs her work and co-runs the creative showcase event Words Per Minute in Glasgow. Anneliese is writer-in-residence at HMP Edinburgh, and is currently finishing a PhD in Creative Writing at the University of Glasgow.

**Kevin MacNeil** is an award-winning poet, playwright and bestselling novelist. His books include A Method Actor's Guide to Jekyll and Hyde, The Stornoway Way, and Love and Zen in the Outer Hebrides. He has held a number of prestigious writing residencies in Europe and he cycled four countries in a dozen cycling days for two cancer charities (on a fixed-gear bike), a feat documented by a film crew and a forthcoming book.

**Duncan McLean** was born in Fraserburgh and lives in Stenness. The National Theatre of Scotland toured his musical show 'Long Gone Lonesome' in 2009 and 2010.

**Aidan Moffat** was born in Falkirk in 1973. He has been writing and recording music since 1996, including ten years in Arab Strap (disbanded in 2006), a few years as L. Pierre (horizontal instrumentals), a spoken word album, a solo album, and lots of obscure ephemera of varying quality.

**Daibhidh Martin** is a writer and director from the Isle of Lewis. He was An Lanntair Writer in residence in 2007 and has had short stories and poetry published in various magazines and anthologies. The story, Omu Prin & Me is part of a novel, which he is currently writing.

**Colette Paul**'s debut short-story collection was "Whoever You Choose to Love." A specialist in short form, she won the Royal Society of Authors Short Story Prize 2005 and has had her work serialised on Radio 4. She teaches creative writing at Anglia Ruskin University and her academic work explores the framework of narratology.

**Suhayl Saadi** is based in Scotland and is obsessed with history, music,minutiae... and doors. His latest novel is 'Joseph's Box' (Two Ravens Press,2009). Various novellas and novelettes have been published on the web. Other books include 'Psychoraag', 'The White Cliffs', 'The Burning Mirror' and 'The Snake'.

**Tawona Sitholé** is a 36 year-old writer and musician, from Zimbabwe. He has been living in Glasgow for over ten years. He is the co-founder of Seeds of Thought creative group, which aims to promote the sharing of cultures through the arts. His work involves writing, performing, organising events, educating and facilitating.

**Ryan Van Winkle** is Reader in Residence at the Scottish Poetry Library and Edinburgh City Libraries. He runs a monthly "Literary Cabaret" called The Golden Hour and is an Editor at Forest Publications. His work has appeared in New Writing Scotland, The American Poetry Review, AGNI and Northwords Now. In 2010 he won Salt's Crashaw Prize and his first collection, Tomorrow We Will Live Here, will be released in Novmber. He lives in Edinburgh but is still an American.

**Allan Wilson** is a writer from Glasgow. He writes short stories, novels and plays. He was selected to appear in 'The Year of Open Doors' having been selected from the open submissions process.

## Publisher's Acknowledgements

The Publisher would like to thank the following people for their assistance and support in the creation of this anthology:

Gillian Tasker
David Flood
Lewis Irvine
Cameron Steel
Kirsteen Connor
Craig Lamont
Caragh Bailie
Aly Barr @ Scottish Arts Council
Sarah Scace @ PSYBT Glasgow
Luciano Rossi
Alun Woodward & Chemikal Underground Records
Professor David Goldie
Chris Buckland
Anne Buckland
Rachael Gallacher
Tommy Adams
Tom Arthur
Graeme West
John-James McDougall
Daniel Verwer
The University of Strathclyde English Studies Department
The Edinburgh International Book Festival
Platform, Glasgow
All institutions who supported our open submission competition
Our editor Dr. Rodge Glass & all the writers who contributed to this collection.

CHEMIKAL UNDERGROUND RECORDS
GLASGOW, SCOTLAND
EST. 1995

Audiobook version of this book is available in association
with Chemikal Underground Records.

www.chemikal.co.uk

www.cargopublishing.com

Also available on iTunes

www.cargopublishing.com

Sign up for free online to get a free personal blog, discussion forums, podcasts and a world of interviews and information on our writers.